Dynamic Programming
and Markov Processes

Dynamic Programming and Markov Processes

RONALD A. HOWARD

The M.I.T. Press
Massachusetts Institute of Technology
Cambridge, Massachusetts

Copyright © 1960
by
The Massachusetts Institute of Technology

All Rights Reserved
This book or any part thereof must not be reproduced in any form without the written permission of the publisher.

Seventh Printing, January 1972

ISBN 0 262 08009 5 (hardcover)

Library of Congress Catalog Card Number: 60-11030
Printed in the United States of America

Preface

This monograph is the outgrowth of an Sc.D. thesis submitted to the Department of Electrical Engineering, M.I.T., in June, 1958. It contains most of the results of that document, subsequent extensions, and sufficient introductory material to afford the interested technical reader a complete understanding of the subject matter.

The monograph was stimulated by widespread interest in dynamic programming as a method for the solution of sequential problems. This material has been used as part of a graduate course in systems engineering and operations research offered in the Electrical Engineering Department of M.I.T. As a result, the present text emphasizes above all else clarity of presentation at the graduate level. It is hoped that it will find use both as collateral reading in graduate and advanced undergraduate courses in operations research, and as a reference for professionals who are interested in the Markov process as a system model.

The thesis from which this work evolved could not have been written without the advice and encouragement of Professors Philip M. Morse and George E. Kimball. Professor Morse aroused my interest in this area; Professor Kimball provided countless helpful suggestions that guided my thinking on basic problems. Conversations with Professors Samuel J. Mason and Bernard Widrow and with Dr. Jerome D. Herniter were also extremely profitable.

The final text was carefully reviewed by Dr. Robert L. Barringer, to whom I owe great appreciation. He and his colleagues at the Operations Research Group of Arthur D. Little, Inc., have continually offered sympathy and encouragement.

PREFACE

This work was done in part at the Massachusetts Institute of Technology Computation Center, Cambridge, Massachusetts, and was supported in part by the Research Laboratory of Electronics.

RONALD A. HOWARD

Cambridge, Massachusetts
February, 1960

Contents

PREFACE		v
INTRODUCTION		1
CHAPTER 1	Markov Processes	3
	The Toymaker Example—State Probabilities	4
	The z-Transformation	7
	z-Transform Analysis of Markov Processes	9
	Transient, Multichain, and Periodic Behavior	12
CHAPTER 2	Markov Processes with Rewards	17
	Solution by Recurrence Relation	17
	The Toymaker Example	18
	z-Transform Analysis of the Markov Process with Rewards	21
	Asymptotic Behavior	22
CHAPTER 3	The Solution of the Sequential Decision Process by Value Iteration	26
	Introduction of Alternatives	26
	The Toymaker's Problem Solved by Value Iteration	28
	Evaluation of the Value-Iteration Approach	30
CHAPTER 4	The Policy-Iteration Method for the Solution of Sequential Decision Processes	32
	The Value-Determination Operation	34
	The Policy-Improvement Routine	37
	The Iteration Cycle	38
	The Toymaker's Problem	39
	A Proof of the Properties of the Policy-Iteration Method	42

CONTENTS

CHAPTER 5 Use of the Policy-Iteration Method in Problems of Taxicab Operation, Baseball, and Automobile Replacement — 44
An Example—Taxicab Operation — 44
A Baseball Problem — 49
The Replacement Problem — 54

CHAPTER 6 The Policy-Iteration Method for Multiple-Chain Processes — 60
The Value-Determination Operation — 61
The Policy-Improvement Routine — 63
A Multichain Example — 65
Properties of the Iteration Cycle — 69

CHAPTER 7 The Sequential Decision Process with Discounting — 76
The Sequential Decision Process with Discounting Solved by Value Iteration — 79
The Value-Determination Operation — 81
The Policy-Improvement Routine — 83
An Example — 84
Proof of the Properties of the Iteration Cycle — 86
The Sensitivity of the Optimal Policy to the Discount Factor — 87
The Automobile Problem with Discounting — 89
Summary — 91

CHAPTER 8 The Continuous-Time Decision Process — 92
The Continuous-Time Markov Process — 92
The Solution of Continuous-Time Markov Processes by Laplace Transformation — 94
The Continuous-Time Markov Process with Rewards — 99
The Continuous-Time Decision Problem — 104
The Value-Determination Operation — 106
The Policy-Improvement Routine — 107
Completely Ergodic Processes — 109
The Foreman's Dilemma — 111
Computational Considerations — 112
The Continuous-Time Decision Process with Discounting — 114
Policy Improvement — 116
An Example — 119
Comparison with Discrete-Time Case — 120

CHAPTER 9 Conclusion — 123

APPENDIX: The Relationship of Transient to Recurrent Behavior — 127

REFERENCES — 133

INDEX — 135

Introduction

The systems engineer or operations researcher is often faced with devising models for operational systems. The systems usually contain both probabilistic and decision-making features, so that we should expect the resultant model to be quite complex and analytically intractable. This has indeed been the case for the majority of models that have been proposed. The exposition of dynamic programming by Richard Bellman[1] gave hope to those engaged in the analysis of complex systems, but this hope was diminished by the realization that more problems could be formulated by this technique than could be solved. Schemes that seemed quite reasonable often ran into computational difficulties that were not easily circumvented.

The intent of this work is to provide an analytic structure for a decision-making system that is at the same time both general enough to be descriptive and yet computationally feasible. It is based on the Markov process as a system model, and uses an iterative technique similar to dynamic programming as its optimization method.

We begin with a discussion of discrete-time Markov processes in Chapter 1 and then add generalizations of the model as we progress. These generalizations include the addition of economic rewards in Chapter 2 and the introduction of the decision process in Chapter 3.

The policy-iteration method for the solution of decision processes with simple probabilistic structures is discussed in Chapter 4 and then examples are presented in Chapter 5. Chapter 6 introduces the case of more complicated probabilistic structures, while Chapter 7 presents the extension of the model to the case where the discounting of future rewards is important. Chapter 8 generalizes all the preceding chapters to continuous-time rather than discrete-time Markov processes. Finally, Chapter 9 contains a few concluding remarks.

It is unfortunate that the nature of the work prevents discussion of the linear programming formulation of the policy-optimization scheme, but this very interesting viewpoint will have to be postponed to another time. Readers who are familiar with linear programming will in any event be able to see familiar structures in the linear forms with which we deal.

1

Markov Processes

A Markov process is a mathematical model that is useful in the study of complex systems. The basic concepts of the Markov process are those of "state" of a system and state "transition." We say that a system occupies a state when it is completely described by the values of variables that define the state. A system makes state transitions when its describing variables change from the values specified for one state to those specified for another.

A graphic example of a Markov process is presented by a frog in a lily pond. As time goes by, the frog jumps from one lily pad to another according to his whim of the moment. The state of the system is the number of the pad currently occupied by the frog; the state transition is of course his leap. If the number of lily pads is finite, then we have a finite-state process. All our future remarks will be confined to such a process.

If we focus our attention on the state transitions of the system and merely index the transitions in time, then we may profitably think of the system as a discrete-time process. If the time between transitions is a random variable that is of interest, then we may consider the system to be a continuous-time process. Further discussion of this latter case will occur in Chapter 8.

To study the discrete-time process, we must specify the probabilistic nature of the state transition. It is convenient to assume that the time between transitions is a constant. Suppose that there are N states in the system numbered from 1 to N. If the system is a simple Markov process, then the probability of a transition to state j during the next time interval, given that the system now occupies state i, is a function only of i and j and not of any history of the system before its arrival in i. In other words, we may specify a set of conditional probabilities p_{ij} that a system which now occupies state i will occupy state j after its next transition. Since the system must be in some state after its next transition,

$$\sum_{j=1}^{N} p_{ij} = 1$$

where the probability that the system will remain in i, p_{ii}, has been included. Since the p_{ij} are probabilities,

$$0 \leqslant p_{ij} \leqslant 1$$

The Toymaker Example—State Probabilities

A very simple example of a discrete-time Markov process of the type we have defined can be thought of as the toymaker's process. The toymaker is involved in the novelty toy business. He may be in either of two states. He is in the first state if the toy he is currently producing has found great favor with the public. He is in the second state if his toy is out of favor. Let us suppose that when he is in state 1 there is 50 per cent chance of his remaining in state 1 at the end of the following week and, consequently, a 50 per cent chance of an unfortunate transition to state 2. When he is in state 2, he experiments with new toys, and he may return to state 1 after a week with probability $\frac{2}{5}$ or remain unprofitable in state 2 with probability $\frac{3}{5}$. Thus $p_{11} = \frac{1}{2}$, $p_{12} = \frac{1}{2}$, $p_{21} = \frac{2}{5}$, $p_{22} = \frac{3}{5}$. In matrix form we have

$$\mathbf{P} = [p_{ij}] = \begin{bmatrix} \frac{1}{2} & \frac{1}{2} \\ \frac{2}{5} & \frac{3}{5} \end{bmatrix}$$

A corresponding transition diagram of the system showing the states and transition probabilities in graphical form is

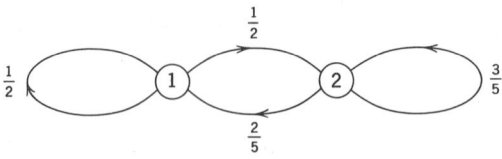

The transition matrix $\mathbf{P}$ is thus a complete description of the Markov process. The rows of this matrix sum to 1, and it is composed of non-negative elements that are not greater than 1; such a matrix is called a

THE TOYMAKER EXAMPLE—STATE PROBABILITIES

stochastic matrix. We make use of this matrix to answer all questions about the process. We may wish to know, for example, the probability that the toymaker will be in state 1 after n weeks if we know he is in state 1 at the beginning of the n-week period. To answer this and other questions, we define a state probability $\pi_i(n)$, the probability that the system will occupy state i after n transitions if its state at $n = 0$ is known. It follows that

$$\sum_{i=1}^{N} \pi_i(n) = 1 \tag{1.1}$$

$$\pi_j(n+1) = \sum_{i=1}^{N} \pi_i(n) p_{ij} \qquad n = 0, 1, 2, \cdots \tag{1.2}$$

If we define a row vector of state probabilities $\pi(n)$ with components $\pi_i(n)$, then

$$\pi(n+1) = \pi(n)\mathbf{P} \qquad n = 0, 1, 2, \cdots \tag{1.3}$$

Since by recursion

$$\pi(1) = \pi(0)\mathbf{P}$$
$$\pi(2) = \pi(1)\mathbf{P} = \pi(0)\mathbf{P}^2$$
$$\pi(3) = \pi(2)\mathbf{P} = \pi(0)\mathbf{P}^3$$

in general,

$$\pi(n) = \pi(0)\mathbf{P}^n \qquad n = 0, 1, 2, \cdots \tag{1.4}$$

Thus it is possible to find the probability that the system occupies each of its states after n moves, $\pi(n)$, by postmultiplying the initial-state probability vector $\pi(0)$ by the nth power of the transition matrix $\mathbf{P}$.

Let us illustrate these relations by applying them to the toymaking process. If the toymaker starts with a successful toy, then $\pi_1(0) = 1$ and $\pi_2(0) = 0$, so that $\pi(0) = [1 \quad 0]$. Therefore, from Eq. 1.3,

$$\pi(1) = \pi(0)\mathbf{P} = \begin{bmatrix} 1 & 0 \end{bmatrix} \begin{bmatrix} \tfrac{1}{2} & \tfrac{1}{2} \\ \tfrac{2}{5} & \tfrac{3}{5} \end{bmatrix}$$

and

$$\pi(1) = \begin{bmatrix} \tfrac{1}{2} & \tfrac{1}{2} \end{bmatrix}$$

After one week, the toymaker is equally likely to be successful or unsuccessful. After two weeks,

$$\pi(2) = \pi(1)\mathbf{P} = \begin{bmatrix} \tfrac{1}{2} & \tfrac{1}{2} \end{bmatrix} \begin{bmatrix} \tfrac{1}{2} & \tfrac{1}{2} \\ \tfrac{2}{5} & \tfrac{3}{5} \end{bmatrix}$$

and

$$\pi(2) = \begin{bmatrix} \tfrac{9}{20} & \tfrac{11}{20} \end{bmatrix}$$

so that the toymaker is slightly more likely to be unsuccessful.

After three weeks, $\pi(3) = \pi(2)\mathbf{P} = [\frac{89}{200}\ \frac{111}{200}]$, and the probability of occupying each state is little changed from the values after two weeks. Note that since

$$\mathbf{P}^3 = \begin{bmatrix} \frac{89}{200} & \frac{111}{200} \\ \frac{111}{250} & \frac{139}{250} \end{bmatrix}$$

$\pi(3)$ could have been obtained directly from $\pi(3) = \pi(0)\mathbf{P}^3$.

An interesting tendency appears if we calculate $\pi_i(n)$ as a function of n as shown in Table 1.1.

Table 1.1. Successive State Probabilities of Toymaker Starting with a Successful Toy

$n =$	0	1	2	3	4	5	...
$\pi_1(n)$	1	0.5	0.45	0.445	0.4445	0.44445	...
$\pi_2(n)$	0	0.5	0.55	0.555	0.5555	0.55555	...

It appears as if $\pi_1(n)$ is approaching $\frac{4}{9}$ and $\pi_2(n)$ is approaching $\frac{5}{9}$ as n becomes very large. If the toymaker starts with an unsuccessful toy, so that $\pi_1(0) = 0$, $\pi_2(0) = 1$, then the table for $\pi_i(n)$ becomes Table 1.2.

Table 1.2. Successive State Probabilities of Toymaker Starting without a Successful Toy

$n =$	0	1	2	3	4	5	...
$\pi_1(n)$	0	0.4	0.44	0.444	0.4444	0.44444	...
$\pi_2(n)$	1	0.6	0.56	0.556	0.5556	0.55556	...

For this case, $\pi_1(n)$ again appears to approach $\frac{4}{9}$ for large n, while $\pi_2(n)$ approaches $\frac{5}{9}$. The state-occupancy probabilities thus appear to be independent of the starting state of the system if the number of state transitions is large. Many Markov processes exhibit this property. We shall designate as a completely ergodic process any Markov process whose limiting state probability distribution is independent of starting conditions. We shall investigate in a later discussion those Markov processes whose state-occupancy probabilities for large numbers of transitions are dependent upon the starting state of the system.

For completely ergodic Markov processes, we may define a quantity π_i as the probability that the system occupies the ith state after a large number of moves. The row vector* π with components π_i is thus the limit as n approaches infinity of $\pi(n)$; it is called the vector of limiting

---

* $\pi(n)$ and π are the only row vectors that we shall consider in our work; other vectors will be column vectors.

THE TOYMAKER EXAMPLE—STATE PROBABILITIES

stochastic matrix. We make use of this matrix to answer all questions about the process. We may wish to know, for example, the probability that the toymaker will be in state 1 after n weeks if we know he is in state 1 at the beginning of the n-week period. To answer this and other questions, we define a state probability $\pi_i(n)$, the probability that the system will occupy state i after n transitions if its state at $n = 0$ is known. It follows that

$$\sum_{i=1}^{N} \pi_i(n) = 1 \tag{1.1}$$

$$\pi_j(n+1) = \sum_{i=1}^{N} \pi_i(n) p_{ij} \qquad n = 0, 1, 2, \cdots \tag{1.2}$$

If we define a row vector of state probabilities $\boldsymbol{\pi}(n)$ with components $\pi_i(n)$, then

$$\boldsymbol{\pi}(n+1) = \boldsymbol{\pi}(n)\mathbf{P} \qquad n = 0, 1, 2, \cdots \tag{1.3}$$

Since by recursion

$$\boldsymbol{\pi}(1) = \boldsymbol{\pi}(0)\mathbf{P}$$
$$\boldsymbol{\pi}(2) = \boldsymbol{\pi}(1)\mathbf{P} = \boldsymbol{\pi}(0)\mathbf{P}^2$$
$$\boldsymbol{\pi}(3) = \boldsymbol{\pi}(2)\mathbf{P} = \boldsymbol{\pi}(0)\mathbf{P}^3$$

in general,

$$\boldsymbol{\pi}(n) = \boldsymbol{\pi}(0)\mathbf{P}^n \qquad n = 0, 1, 2, \cdots \tag{1.4}$$

Thus it is possible to find the probability that the system occupies each of its states after n moves, $\boldsymbol{\pi}(n)$, by postmultiplying the initial-state probability vector $\boldsymbol{\pi}(0)$ by the nth power of the transition matrix $\mathbf{P}$.

Let us illustrate these relations by applying them to the toymaking process. If the toymaker starts with a successful toy, then $\pi_1(0) = 1$ and $\pi_2(0) = 0$, so that $\boldsymbol{\pi}(0) = [1 \quad 0]$. Therefore, from Eq. 1.3,

$$\boldsymbol{\pi}(1) = \boldsymbol{\pi}(0)\mathbf{P} = [1 \quad 0] \begin{bmatrix} \frac{1}{2} & \frac{1}{2} \\ \frac{2}{5} & \frac{3}{5} \end{bmatrix}$$

and

$$\boldsymbol{\pi}(1) = [\tfrac{1}{2} \quad \tfrac{1}{2}]$$

After one week, the toymaker is equally likely to be successful or unsuccessful. After two weeks,

$$\boldsymbol{\pi}(2) = \boldsymbol{\pi}(1)\mathbf{P} = [\tfrac{1}{2} \quad \tfrac{1}{2}] \begin{bmatrix} \frac{1}{2} & \frac{1}{2} \\ \frac{2}{5} & \frac{3}{5} \end{bmatrix}$$

and

$$\boldsymbol{\pi}(2) = [\tfrac{9}{20} \quad \tfrac{11}{20}]$$

so that the toymaker is slightly more likely to be unsuccessful.

After three weeks, $\pi(3) = \pi(2)\mathbf{P} = [\frac{89}{200} \quad \frac{111}{200}]$, and the probability of occupying each state is little changed from the values after two weeks. Note that since

$$\mathbf{P}^3 = \begin{bmatrix} \frac{89}{200} & \frac{111}{200} \\ \frac{111}{250} & \frac{139}{250} \end{bmatrix}$$

$\pi(3)$ could have been obtained directly from $\pi(3) = \pi(0)\mathbf{P}^3$.

An interesting tendency appears if we calculate $\pi_i(n)$ as a function of n as shown in Table 1.1.

Table 1.1. Successive State Probabilities of Toymaker Starting with a Successful Toy

$n =$	0	1	2	3	4	5	...
$\pi_1(n)$	1	0.5	0.45	0.445	0.4445	0.44445	...
$\pi_2(n)$	0	0.5	0.55	0.555	0.5555	0.55555	...

It appears as if $\pi_1(n)$ is approaching $\frac{4}{9}$ and $\pi_2(n)$ is approaching $\frac{5}{9}$ as n becomes very large. If the toymaker starts with an unsuccessful toy, so that $\pi_1(0) = 0$, $\pi_2(0) = 1$, then the table for $\pi_i(n)$ becomes Table 1.2.

Table 1.2. Successive State Probabilities of Toymaker Starting without a Successful Toy

$n =$	0	1	2	3	4	5	...
$\pi_1(n)$	0	0.4	0.44	0.444	0.4444	0.44444	...
$\pi_2(n)$	1	0.6	0.56	0.556	0.5556	0.55556	...

For this case, $\pi_1(n)$ again appears to approach $\frac{4}{9}$ for large n, while $\pi_2(n)$ approaches $\frac{5}{9}$. The state-occupancy probabilities thus appear to be independent of the starting state of the system if the number of state transitions is large. Many Markov processes exhibit this property. We shall designate as a completely ergodic process any Markov process whose limiting state probability distribution is independent of starting conditions. We shall investigate in a later discussion those Markov processes whose state-occupancy probabilities for large numbers of transitions are dependent upon the starting state of the system.

For completely ergodic Markov processes, we may define a quantity π_i as the probability that the system occupies the ith state after a large number of moves. The row vector* π with components π_i is thus the limit as n approaches infinity of $\pi(n)$; it is called the vector of limiting

---

* $\pi(n)$ and π are the only row vectors that we shall consider in our work; other vectors will be column vectors.

or absolute state probabilities. It follows from Eq. 1.3 that the vector $\boldsymbol{\pi}$ must obey the equation

$$\boldsymbol{\pi} = \boldsymbol{\pi} \mathbf{P} \tag{1.5}$$

and, of course, the sum of the components of $\boldsymbol{\pi}$ must be 1.

$$\sum_{i=1}^{N} \pi_i = 1 \tag{1.6}$$

We may use Eqs. 1.5 and 1.6 to find the limiting state probabilities for any process. For the toymaker example, Eq. 1.5 yields

$$\pi_1 = \tfrac{1}{2}\pi_1 + \tfrac{2}{5}\pi_2$$
$$\pi_2 = \tfrac{1}{2}\pi_1 + \tfrac{3}{5}\pi_2$$

whereas Eq. 1.6 becomes $\pi_1 + \pi_2 = 1$.

The three equations for the two unknowns π_1 and π_2 have the unique solution $\pi_1 = \tfrac{4}{9}$, $\pi_2 = \tfrac{5}{9}$. These are, of course, the same values for the limiting state probabilities that we inferred from our tables of $\pi_i(n)$. In many applications the limiting state probabilities are the only quantities of interest. It may be sufficient to know, for example, that our toymaker is fortunate enough to have a successful toy $\tfrac{4}{9}$ of the time and is unfortunate $\tfrac{5}{9}$ of the time. The difficulty involved in finding the limiting state probabilities is precisely that of solving a set of N linear simultaneous equations. We must remember, however, that the quantities π_i are a sufficient description of the process only if enough transitions have occurred for the memory of starting position to be lost. In the following section, we shall gain more insight into the behavior of the process during the transient period when the state probabilities are approaching their limiting values.

The z-Transformation

For the study of transient behavior and for theoretical convenience, it is useful to study the Markov process from the point of view of the generating function or, as we shall call it, the z-transform. Consider a time function $f(n)$ that takes on arbitrary values $f(0), f(1), f(2)$, and so on, at nonnegative, discrete, integrally spaced points of time and that is zero for negative time. Such a time function is shown in Fig. 1.1. For time functions that do not increase in magnitude with n faster than a geometric sequence, it is possible to define a z-transform $f(z)$ such that

$$f(z) = \sum_{n=0}^{\infty} f(n) z^n \tag{1.7}$$

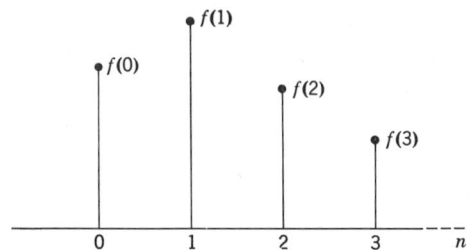

Fig. 1.1. An arbitrary discrete-time function.

The relationship between $f(n)$ and its transform $f(z)$ is unique; each time function has only one transform, and the inverse transformation of the transform will produce once more the original time function. The z-transformation is useful in Markov processes because the probability transients in Markov processes are geometric sequences. The z-transform provides us with a closed-form expression for such sequences.

Let us find the z-transforms of the typical time functions that we shall soon encounter. Consider first the step function

$$f(n) = \begin{cases} 1 & n = 0, 1, 2, 3, \cdots \\ 0 & n < 0 \end{cases}$$

The z-transform is

$$f(z) = \sum_{n=0}^{\infty} f(n) z^n = 1 + z + z^2 + z^3 + \cdots \qquad \text{or } f(z) = \frac{1}{1-z}$$

For the geometric sequence $f(n) = \alpha^n$, $n \geq 0$,

$$f(z) = \sum_{n=0}^{\infty} f(n) z^n = \sum_{n=0}^{\infty} (\alpha z)^n \qquad \text{or } f(z) = \frac{1}{1-\alpha z}$$

Note that if

$$f(z) = \sum_{n=0}^{\infty} \alpha^n z^n$$

then

$$\frac{d}{dz} f(z) = \sum_{n=0}^{\infty} n \alpha^n z^{n-1}$$

and

$$\sum_{n=0}^{\infty} n \alpha^n z^n = z \frac{d}{dz} f(z) = z \frac{d}{dz} \left(\frac{1}{1-\alpha z} \right) = \frac{\alpha z}{(1-\alpha z)^2}$$

Thus we have obtained as a derived result that, if the time function we are dealing with is $f(n) = n\alpha^n$, its z-transform is $f(z) = \alpha z/(1-\alpha z)^2$.

z-TRANSFORM ANALYSIS OF MARKOV PROCESSES

From these and other easily derived results, we may compile the table of z-transforms shown as Table 1.3. In particular, note that, if a time function $f(n)$ with transform $f(z)$ is shifted to the right one unit so as to become $f(n + 1)$, then the transform of the shifted function is

$$\sum_{n=0}^{\infty} f(n+1)z^n = \sum_{m=1}^{\infty} f(m)z^{m-1} = z^{-1}[f(z) - f(0)]$$

The reader should become familiar with the results of Table 1.3 because they will be used extensively in examples and proofs.

Table 1.3. z-TRANSFORM PAIRS

Time Function for $n \geq 0$	z-Transform
$f(n)$	$f(z)$
$f_1(n) + f_2(n)$	$f_1(z) + f_2(z)$
$kf(n)$ (k is a constant)	$kf(z)$
$f(n-1)$	$zf(z)$
$f(n+1)$	$z^{-1}[f(z) - f(0)]$
α^n	$\dfrac{1}{1 - \alpha z}$
1 (unit step)	$\dfrac{1}{1 - z}$
$n\alpha^n$	$\dfrac{\alpha z}{(1 - \alpha z)^2}$
n (unit ramp)	$\dfrac{z}{(1 - z)^2}$
$\alpha^n f(n)$	$f(\alpha z)$

z-Transform Analysis of Markov Processes

We shall now use the z-transform to analyze Markov processes. It is possible to take the z-transform of vectors and matrices by taking the z-transform of each component of the array. If the transform of Eq. 1.3 is taken in this sense, and if the vector z-transform of the vector $\pi(n)$ is given the symbol $\mathbf{\Pi}(z)$, then we obtain

$$z^{-1}[\mathbf{\Pi}(z) - \pi(0)] = \mathbf{\Pi}(z)\mathbf{P} \qquad (1.8)$$

Through rearrangement we have

$$\mathbf{\Pi}(z) - z\mathbf{\Pi}(z)\mathbf{P} = \pi(0)$$
$$\mathbf{\Pi}(z)(\mathbf{I} - z\mathbf{P}) = \pi(0)$$

and finally

$$\mathbf{\Pi}(z) = \pi(0)(\mathbf{I} - z\mathbf{P})^{-1} \qquad (1.9)$$

In this expression $\mathbf{I}$ is the identity matrix. The transform of the state probability vector is thus equal to the initial-state-probability vector postmultiplied by the inverse of the matrix $\mathbf{I} - z\mathbf{P}$; the inverse of $\mathbf{I} - z\mathbf{P}$ will always exist. Note that the solution to all transient problems is contained in the matrix $(\mathbf{I} - z\mathbf{P})^{-1}$. To obtain the complete solution to any transient problem, all we must do is to weight the rows of $(\mathbf{I} - z\mathbf{P})^{-1}$ by the initial state probabilities, sum, and then take the inverse transform of each element in the result.

Let us investigate the toymaker's problem by z-transformation. For this case

$$\mathbf{P} = \begin{bmatrix} \tfrac{1}{2} & \tfrac{1}{2} \\ \tfrac{2}{5} & \tfrac{3}{5} \end{bmatrix}$$

so that

$$(\mathbf{I} - z\mathbf{P}) = \begin{bmatrix} 1 - \tfrac{1}{2}z & -\tfrac{1}{2}z \\ -\tfrac{2}{5}z & 1 - \tfrac{3}{5}z \end{bmatrix}$$

and

$$(\mathbf{I} - z\mathbf{P})^{-1} = \begin{bmatrix} \dfrac{1 - \tfrac{3}{5}z}{(1-z)(1 - \tfrac{1}{10}z)} & \dfrac{\tfrac{1}{2}z}{(1-z)(1 - \tfrac{1}{10}z)} \\ \dfrac{\tfrac{2}{5}z}{(1-z)(1 - \tfrac{1}{10}z)} & \dfrac{1 - \tfrac{1}{2}z}{(1-z)(1 - \tfrac{1}{10}z)} \end{bmatrix}$$

Each element of $(\mathbf{I} - z\mathbf{P})^{-1}$ is a function of z with a factorable denominator $(1-z)(1 - \tfrac{1}{10}z)$. By partial-fraction expansion[2] we can express each element as the sum of two terms: one with denominator $1 - z$ and one with denominator $1 - \tfrac{1}{10}z$. The $(\mathbf{I} - z\mathbf{P})^{-1}$ matrix now becomes

$$(\mathbf{I} - z\mathbf{P})^{-1} = \begin{bmatrix} \dfrac{\tfrac{4}{9}}{1-z} + \dfrac{\tfrac{5}{9}}{1 - \tfrac{1}{10}z} & \dfrac{\tfrac{5}{9}}{1-z} + \dfrac{-\tfrac{5}{9}}{1 - \tfrac{1}{10}z} \\ \dfrac{\tfrac{4}{9}}{1-z} + \dfrac{-\tfrac{4}{9}}{1 - \tfrac{1}{10}z} & \dfrac{\tfrac{5}{9}}{1-z} + \dfrac{\tfrac{4}{9}}{1 - \tfrac{1}{10}z} \end{bmatrix}$$

$$(\mathbf{I} - z\mathbf{P})^{-1} = \dfrac{1}{1-z}\begin{bmatrix} \tfrac{4}{9} & \tfrac{5}{9} \\ \tfrac{4}{9} & \tfrac{5}{9} \end{bmatrix} + \dfrac{1}{1 - \tfrac{1}{10}z}\begin{bmatrix} \tfrac{5}{9} & -\tfrac{5}{9} \\ -\tfrac{4}{9} & \tfrac{4}{9} \end{bmatrix}$$

Let the matrix $\mathbf{H}(n)$ be the inverse transform of $(\mathbf{I} - z\mathbf{P})^{-1}$ on an element-by-element basis. Then from Table 1.3, we see that

$$\mathbf{H}(n) = \begin{bmatrix} \tfrac{4}{9} & \tfrac{5}{9} \\ \tfrac{4}{9} & \tfrac{5}{9} \end{bmatrix} + (\tfrac{1}{10})^n \begin{bmatrix} \tfrac{5}{9} & -\tfrac{5}{9} \\ -\tfrac{4}{9} & \tfrac{4}{9} \end{bmatrix}$$

and finally by taking the inverse transform of Eq. 1.9

$$\boldsymbol{\pi}(n) = \boldsymbol{\pi}(0)\mathbf{H}(n) \qquad (1.10)$$

By comparison with Eq. 1.4 we see that $\mathbf{H}(n) = \mathbf{P}^n$, and that we have found a convenient way to calculate the nth power of the transition-probability matrix in closed form. The state-probability vector at time n can thus be found by postmultiplying the initial-state-probability vector by the response matrix $\mathbf{H}(n)$. The ijth element of the matrix $\mathbf{H}(n)$ represents the probability that the system will occupy state j at time n, given that it occupied state i at time $n = 0$. If the toymaker starts in the successful state 1, then $\boldsymbol{\pi}(0) = [1 \quad 0]$ and $\boldsymbol{\pi}(n) = [\tfrac{4}{9} \quad \tfrac{5}{9}] + (\tfrac{1}{10})^n [\tfrac{5}{9} \quad -\tfrac{5}{9}]$ or $\pi_1(n) = \tfrac{4}{9} + \tfrac{5}{9}(\tfrac{1}{10})^n$, $\pi_2(n) = \tfrac{5}{9} - \tfrac{5}{9}(\tfrac{1}{10})^n$.

Note that the expressions for $\pi_1(n)$ and $\pi_2(n)$ are exact analytic representations for the state probabilities found in Table 1.1 by matrix multiplication. Note further that as n becomes very large $\pi_1(n)$ tends to $\tfrac{4}{9}$ and $\pi_2(n)$ tends to $\tfrac{5}{9}$; they approach the limiting state probabilities of the process.

If the toymaker starts in state 2, then $\boldsymbol{\pi}(0) = [0 \quad 1]$, $\boldsymbol{\pi}(n) = [\tfrac{4}{9} \quad \tfrac{5}{9}] + (\tfrac{1}{10})^n [-\tfrac{4}{9} \quad \tfrac{4}{9}]$, so that $\pi_1(n) = \tfrac{4}{9} - \tfrac{4}{9}(\tfrac{1}{10})^n$ and $\pi_2(n) = \tfrac{5}{9} + \tfrac{4}{9}(\tfrac{1}{10})^n$. We have now obtained analytic forms for the data in Table 1.2. Once more we see that for large n the state probabilities become the limiting state probabilities of the process.

It is possible to make some general statements about the form that $\mathbf{H}(n)$ may take. First it will always have among its component matrices at least one that is a stochastic matrix and that arises from a term of $(\mathbf{I} - z\mathbf{P})^{-1}$ of the form $1/(1-z)$. This statement is equivalent to saying that the determinant of $\mathbf{I} - z\mathbf{P}$ vanishes for $z = 1$ or that a stochastic matrix always has at least one characteristic value equal to 1. If the process is completely ergodic, then there will be exactly one stochastic matrix in $\mathbf{H}(n)$. Furthermore, the rows of this matrix will be identical and will each be the limiting-state-probability vector of the process. We call this portion of $\mathbf{H}(n)$ the steady-state portion and give it the symbol $\mathbf{S}$ since it is not a function of n.

The remainder of the terms of $\mathbf{H}(n)$ represent the transient behavior of the process. These terms are matrices multiplied by coefficients of the form α^n, $n\alpha^n$, $n^2\alpha^n$, and so on. Naturally, $|\alpha|$ must not be greater than 1, for if any α were greater than 1, that component of probability would grow without bound, a situation that is clearly impossible. The transient matrices represent the decreasing geometric sequences of probability components that are typical of Markov processes. The transient component of $\mathbf{H}(n)$ may be given the symbol $\mathbf{T}(n)$ since it is a function of n. Since for completely ergodic processes $|\alpha| < 1$ for all α, the transient component $\mathbf{T}(n)$ vanishes as n becomes very large. The matrices that compose $\mathbf{T}(n)$ are also of interest because they sum to zero across each row. The transient components must sum to zero since they may be considered as perturbations applied to the limiting state probabilities. Matrices that sum to zero across all rows are called differential matrices. Finally, for a completely ergodic process,

$$\mathbf{H}(n) = \mathbf{S} + \mathbf{T}(n) \tag{1.11}$$

where $\mathbf{S}$ is a stochastic matrix all of whose rows are equal to the limiting state-probability vector and where $\mathbf{T}(n)$ is the sum of a number of differential matrices with geometric coefficients that tend to zero as n becomes very large.

Transient, Multichain, and Periodic Behavior

To gain further insight into the Markov process, let us use the z-transform approach to analyze processes that exhibit typical behavior patterns. In the toymaker's problem, both states had a finite probability of occupancy after a large number of transitions. It is possible even in a completely ergodic process for some of the states to have a limiting state probability of zero. Such states are called transient states because we are certain that they will not be occupied after a long time. A two-state problem with a transient state is described by

$$\mathbf{P} = \begin{bmatrix} \frac{3}{4} & \frac{1}{4} \\ 0 & 1 \end{bmatrix}$$

with transition diagram

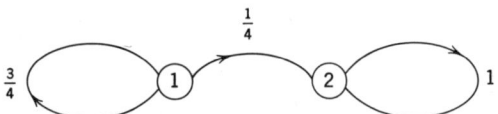

If the system is in state 1, it has probability $\frac{1}{4}$ of making a transition to state 2. However, if a transition to 2 occurs, then the system will remain in 2 for all future time. State 1 is a transient state; state 2 is a trapping state (a state i for which $p_{ii} = 1$).

By applying the z-transform analysis, we find

$$(\mathbf{I} - z\mathbf{P}) = \begin{bmatrix} 1 - \frac{3}{4}z & -\frac{1}{4}z \\ 0 & 1 - z \end{bmatrix}$$

and

$$(\mathbf{I} - z\mathbf{P})^{-1} = \begin{bmatrix} \dfrac{1-z}{(1-z)(1-\frac{3}{4}z)} & \dfrac{\frac{1}{4}z}{(1-z)(1-\frac{3}{4}z)} \\ \dfrac{0}{(1-z)(1-\frac{3}{4}z)} & \dfrac{1-\frac{3}{4}z}{(1-z)(1-\frac{3}{4}z)} \end{bmatrix}$$

TRANSIENT, MULTICHAIN, AND PERIODIC BEHAVIOR

$$(\mathbf{I} - z\mathbf{P})^{-1} = \frac{1}{1-z}\begin{bmatrix} 0 & 1 \\ 0 & 1 \end{bmatrix} + \frac{1}{1-\frac{3}{4}z}\begin{bmatrix} 1 & -1 \\ 0 & 0 \end{bmatrix}$$

Thus

$$\mathbf{H}(n) = \begin{bmatrix} 0 & 1 \\ 0 & 1 \end{bmatrix} + (\tfrac{3}{4})^n \begin{bmatrix} 1 & -1 \\ 0 & 0 \end{bmatrix}$$

If the system is started in state 1 so that $\pi(0) = [1 \ 0]$, then $\pi_1(n) = (\tfrac{3}{4})^n$, $\pi_2(n) = 1 - (\tfrac{3}{4})^n$. If the system is started in state 2 with $\pi(0) = [0 \ 1]$, then naturally $\pi_1(n) = 0$, $\pi_2(n) = 1$. In either case we see that the limiting state probability of state 1 is zero, so our assertion that it is a transient state is correct. Of course the limiting state probabilities could have been determined from Eqs. 1.5 and 1.6 in the manner described earlier.

A transient state need not lead the system into a trapping state. The system may leave a transient state and enter a set of states that are connected by possible transitions in such a way that the system makes jumps within this set of states indefinitely but never jumps outside the set. Such a set of states is called a recurrent chain of the Markov process; every Markov process must have at least one recurrent chain. A Markov process that has only one recurrent chain must be completely ergodic because no matter where the process is started it will end up making jumps among the members of the recurrent chain. However, if a process has two or more recurrent chains, then the completely ergodic property no longer holds, for if the system is started in a state of one chain then it will continue to make transitions within that chain but never to a state of another chain. In this sense, each recurrent chain is a generalized trapping state; once it is entered, it can never be left. We may now think of a transient state as a state that the system occupies before it becomes committed to one of the recurrent chains.

The possibility of many recurrent chains forces us to revise our thinking concerning $\mathbf{S}$, the steady-state component of $\mathbf{H}(n)$. Since the limiting state probability distribution is now dependent on how the system is started, the rows of the stochastic matrix $\mathbf{S}$ are no longer equal. Rather, the ith row of $\mathbf{S}$ represents the limiting state probability distribution that would exist if the system were started in the ith state. The ith row of the $\mathbf{T}(n)$ matrix is as before the set of transient components of the state probability if i is the starting state.

Let us investigate a very simple three-state process with two recurrent chains described by

$$\mathbf{P} = \begin{bmatrix} 1 & 0 & 0 \\ 0 & 1 & 0 \\ \tfrac{1}{3} & \tfrac{1}{3} & \tfrac{1}{3} \end{bmatrix}$$

with the transition diagram

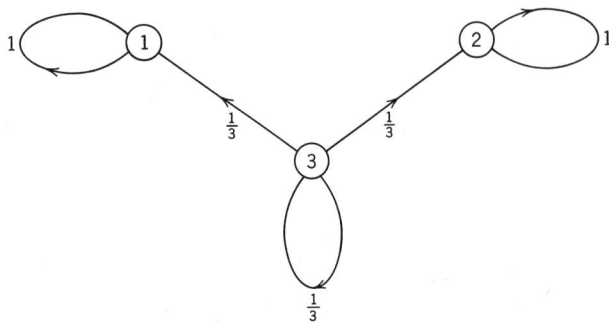

State 1 constitutes one recurrent chain; state 2 the other. Both are trapping states, but the general behavior would be unchanged if each were a collection of connected states. State 3 is a transient state that may lead the system to either of the recurrent chains. To find $\mathbf{H}(n)$ for this process, we first find

$$(\mathbf{I} - z\mathbf{P}) = \begin{bmatrix} 1-z & 0 & 0 \\ 0 & 1-z & 0 \\ -\tfrac{1}{3}z & -\tfrac{1}{3}z & 1-\tfrac{1}{3}z \end{bmatrix}$$

and

$$(\mathbf{I} - z\mathbf{P})^{-1} = \begin{bmatrix} \dfrac{(1-z)(1-\tfrac{1}{3}z)}{(1-z)^2(1-\tfrac{1}{3}z)} & 0 & 0 \\ 0 & \dfrac{(1-z)(1-\tfrac{1}{3}z)}{(1-z)^2(1-\tfrac{1}{3}z)} & 0 \\ \dfrac{(1-z)\tfrac{1}{3}z}{(1-z)^2(1-\tfrac{1}{3}z)} & \dfrac{(1-z)\tfrac{1}{3}z}{(1-z)^2(1-\tfrac{1}{3}z)} & \dfrac{(1-z)^2}{(1-z)^2(1-\tfrac{1}{3}z)} \end{bmatrix}$$

Thus

$$(\mathbf{I} - z\mathbf{P})^{-1} = \dfrac{1}{1-z}\begin{bmatrix} 1 & 0 & 0 \\ 0 & 1 & 0 \\ \tfrac{1}{2} & \tfrac{1}{2} & 0 \end{bmatrix} + \dfrac{1}{1-\tfrac{1}{3}z}\begin{bmatrix} 0 & 0 & 0 \\ 0 & 0 & 0 \\ -\tfrac{1}{2} & -\tfrac{1}{2} & 1 \end{bmatrix}$$

and

$$\mathbf{H}(n) = \begin{bmatrix} 1 & 0 & 0 \\ 0 & 1 & 0 \\ \tfrac{1}{2} & \tfrac{1}{2} & 0 \end{bmatrix} + (\tfrac{1}{3})^n \begin{bmatrix} 0 & 0 & 0 \\ 0 & 0 & 0 \\ -\tfrac{1}{2} & -\tfrac{1}{2} & 1 \end{bmatrix}$$

$$= \quad \mathbf{S} \quad + \quad \mathbf{T}(n)$$

If the system is started in state 1, $\pi_1(n) = 1$, $\pi_2(n) = \pi_3(n) = 0$. If the system is started in state 2, $\pi_1(n) = \pi_3(n) = 0$, $\pi_2(n) = 1$. If the system is started in state 3, $\pi_1(n) = \pi_2(n) = \frac{1}{2}[1 - (\frac{1}{3})^n]$, $\pi_3(n) = (\frac{1}{3})^n$.

We may summarize by saying that if the system is started in state 1 or state 2 it will remain in its starting state indefinitely. If it is started in state 3, it will be after many moves in state 1 with probability $\frac{1}{2}$ and in state 2 with probability $\frac{1}{2}$. These results may be seen directly from the rows of **S** which are, after all, the limiting state probability distributions for each starting condition.

The multichain Markov process is thus treated with ease by z-transformation methods. There is one other case that requires discussion, however, before we may feel at all confident of our knowledge. That is the case of periodic chains. A periodic chain is a recurrent chain with the property that if the system occupies some state at the present time it will be certain to occupy that same state after $p, 2p, 3p, 4p, \cdots$ transitions, where p is an integer describing the periodicity of the system. The simplest periodic system is the two-state system of period 2 with transition matrix

$$\mathbf{P} = \begin{bmatrix} 0 & 1 \\ 1 & 0 \end{bmatrix}$$

and transition diagram

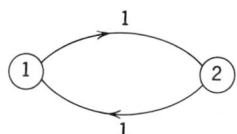

If the system is started in state 1, it will be once more in state 1 after even numbers of transitions and in state 2 after odd numbers of transitions. There is no need for analysis to understand this type of behavior, but let us investigate the results obtained by the transformation method. We have

$$(\mathbf{I} - z\mathbf{P}) = \begin{bmatrix} 1 & -z \\ -z & 1 \end{bmatrix}$$

$$(\mathbf{I} - z\mathbf{P})^{-1} = \begin{bmatrix} \dfrac{1}{(1-z)(1+z)} & \dfrac{z}{(1-z)(1+z)} \\ \dfrac{z}{(1-z)(1+z)} & \dfrac{1}{(1-z)(1+z)} \end{bmatrix}$$

and

$$(\mathbf{I} - z\mathbf{P})^{-1} = \frac{1}{1-z}\begin{bmatrix} \frac{1}{2} & \frac{1}{2} \\ \frac{1}{2} & \frac{1}{2} \end{bmatrix} + \frac{1}{1+z}\begin{bmatrix} \frac{1}{2} & -\frac{1}{2} \\ -\frac{1}{2} & \frac{1}{2} \end{bmatrix}$$

The response matrix $\mathbf{H}(n)$ is thus

$$\mathbf{H}(n) = \begin{bmatrix} \frac{1}{2} & \frac{1}{2} \\ \frac{1}{2} & \frac{1}{2} \end{bmatrix} + (-1)^n \begin{bmatrix} \frac{1}{2} & -\frac{1}{2} \\ -\frac{1}{2} & \frac{1}{2} \end{bmatrix}$$

This $\mathbf{H}(n)$ does represent the solution to the problem because, for example, if the system is started in state 1, $\pi_1(n) = \frac{1}{2}[1 + (-1)^n]$ and $\pi_2(n) = \frac{1}{2}[1 - (-1)^n]$. These expressions produce the same results that we saw intuitively. However, what is to be the interpretation placed on $\mathbf{S}$ and $\mathbf{T}(n)$ in this problem? The matrix $\mathbf{T}(n)$ contains components that do not die away for larger n, but rather continue to oscillate indefinitely. On the other hand, $\mathbf{T}(n)$ can still be considered as a perturbation to the set of limiting state probabilities defined by $\mathbf{S}$. The best interpretation of the limiting state probabilities of $\mathbf{S}$ is that they represent the probability that the system will be found in each of its states at a *time* chosen at random in the future. For periodic processes, the original concept of limiting state probabilities is not relevant since we know the state of the system at all future times. However, in many practical cases, the random-time interpretation introduced above is meaningful and useful. Whenever we consider the limiting state probabilities of a periodic Markov process, we shall use them in this sense. Incidentally, if Eqs. 1.5 and 1.6 are used to find the limiting state probabilities, they yield $\pi_1 = \pi_2 = \frac{1}{2}$, in agreement with our understanding.

We have now investigated the behavior of Markov processes using the mechanism of the z-transform. This particular approach is useful because it circumvents the difficulties that arise because of multiple characteristic values of stochastic matrices. Many otherwise elegant discussions of Markov processes based on matrix theory are markedly complicated by this difficulty. The structure of the transform method can be even more appreciated if use is made of the work that has been done on signal-flow-graph models of Markov processes, but this is beyond our present scope; references 3 and 4 may be useful.

The following chapter will begin the analysis of Markov processes that have economic rewards associated with state transitions.

2

Markov Processes with Rewards

Suppose that an N-state Markov process earns r_{ij} dollars when it makes a transition from state i to state j. We call r_{ij} the "reward" associated with the transition from i to j. The set of rewards for the process may be described by a reward matrix **R** with elements r_{ij}. The rewards need not be in dollars, they could be voltage levels, units of production, or any other physical quantity relevant to the problem. In most of our work, however, we shall find that economic units such as dollars will be the pertinent interpretation.

The Markov process now generates a sequence of rewards as it makes transitions from state to state. The reward is thus a random variable with a probability distribution governed by the probabilistic relations of the Markov process. Recalling our frog pond, we can picture a game where the player receives an amount of money r_{ij} if the frog jumps from pad i to pad j. As some of the r_{ij} might be negative, the player on occasion would have to contribute to the pot.

Solution by Recurrence Relation

One question we might ask concerning this game is: What will be the player's expected winnings in the next n jumps if the frog is now in state i (sitting on the lily pad numbered i)? To answer this question, let us define $v_i(n)$ as the expected total earnings in the next n transitions if the system is now in state i.

Some reflection on this definition allows us to write the recurrence relation

$$v_i(n) = \sum_{j=1}^{N} p_{ij}[r_{ij} + v_j(n-1)] \quad i = 1, 2, \cdots, N \quad n = 1, 2, 3, \cdots \quad (2.1)$$

If the system makes a transition from i to j, it will earn the amount r_{ij} plus the amount it expects to earn if it starts in state j with one move fewer remaining. As shown in Eq. 2.1, these earnings from a transition to j must be weighted by the probability of such a transition, p_{ij}, to obtain the total expected earnings.

Notice that Eq. 2.1 may be written in the form

$$v_i(n) = \sum_{j=1}^{N} p_{ij} r_{ij} + \sum_{j=1}^{N} p_{ij} v_j(n-1)$$
$$i = 1, 2, \cdots, N \quad n = 1, 2, 3, \cdots \quad (2.2)$$

so that if a quantity q_i is defined by

$$q_i = \sum_{j=1}^{N} p_{ij} r_{ij} \quad i = 1, 2, \cdots, N \quad (2.3)$$

Eq. 2.1 takes the form

$$v_i(n) = q_i + \sum_{j=1}^{N} p_{ij} v_j(n-1) \quad i = 1, 2, \cdots, N \quad n = 1, 2, 3, \cdots \quad (2.4)$$

The quantity q_i may be interpreted as the reward to be expected in the next transition out of state i; it will be called the expected immediate reward for state i. In terms of the frog jumping game, q_i is the amount that the player expects to receive from the next jump of the frog if it is now on lily pad i. Rewriting Eq. 2.1 as Eq. 2.4 shows us that it is not necessary to specify both a **P** matrix and an **R** matrix in order to determine the expected earnings of the system. All that is needed is a **P** matrix and a **q** column vector with N components q_i. The reduction in data storage is significant when large problems are to be solved on a digital computer. In vector form, Eq. 2.4 may be written as

$$\mathbf{v}(n) = \mathbf{q} + \mathbf{P}\mathbf{v}(n-1) \quad n = 1, 2, 3, \cdots \quad (2.5)$$

where $\mathbf{v}(n)$ is a column vector with N components $v_i(n)$, called the total-value vector.

The Toymaker Example

To investigate the problem of expected earnings in greater detail, let us add a reward structure to the toymaker's problem. Suppose that

THE TOYMAKER EXAMPLE

when the toymaker has a successful toy (the system is in state 1) and again has a successful toy the following week (the system makes a transition from state 1 to state 1) he earns a reward of 9 units for that week (perhaps $900). Thus r_{11} is equal to 9. If the week has resulted in a transition from unsuccessful to unsuccessful (state 2 to state 2), then the toymaker loses 7 units or $r_{22} = -7$. Finally, if the week has produced a change from unsuccessful to successful or from successful to unsuccessful, the earnings are 3 units, so that $r_{21} = r_{12} = 3$. The reward matrix **R** is thus

$$\mathbf{R} = \begin{bmatrix} 9 & 3 \\ 3 & -7 \end{bmatrix}$$

Recalling that

$$\mathbf{P} = \begin{bmatrix} 0.5 & 0.5 \\ 0.4 & 0.6 \end{bmatrix}$$

we can find **q** from Eq. 2.3:

$$\mathbf{q} = \begin{bmatrix} 6 \\ -3 \end{bmatrix}$$

Inspection of the **q** vector shows that if the toymaker has a successful toy he expects to make 6 units in the following week; if he has no successful toy, the expected loss for the next week is 3 units.

Suppose that the toymaker knows that he is going to go out of business after n weeks. He is interested in determining the amount of money he may expect to make in that time, depending on whether or not he now has a successful toy. The recurrence relations Eq. 2.4 or Eq. 2.5 may be directly applied to this problem, but a set of boundary values $v_i(0)$ must be specified. These quantities represent the expected return the toymaker will receive on the day he ceases operation. If the business is sold to another party, $v_1(0)$, would be the purchase price if the firm had a successful toy on the selling date, and $v_2(0)$ would be the purchase price if the business were not so situated on that day. Arbitrarily, for computational convenience, the boundary values $v_i(0)$ will be set equal to zero in our example.

We may now use Eq. 2.4 to prepare Table 2.1 that shows $v_i(n)$ for each state and for several values of n.

Table 2.1. TOTAL EXPECTED REWARD FOR TOYMAKER AS A FUNCTION OF STATE AND NUMBER OF WEEKS REMAINING

$n =$	0	1	2	3	4	5	...
$v_1(n)$	0	6	7.5	8.55	9.555	10.5555	...
$v_2(n)$	0	−3	−2.4	−1.44	−0.444	0.5556	...

Thus, if the toymaker is four weeks from his shutdown time, he expects to make 9.555 units in the remaining time if he now has a successful toy and to lose 0.444 unit if he does not have one. Note that $v_1(n) - v_2(n)$ seems to be approaching 10 as n becomes large, whereas both $v_1(n) - v_1(n-1)$ and $v_2(n) - v_2(n-1)$ seem to approach the value 1 for large n. In other words, when n is large, having a successful

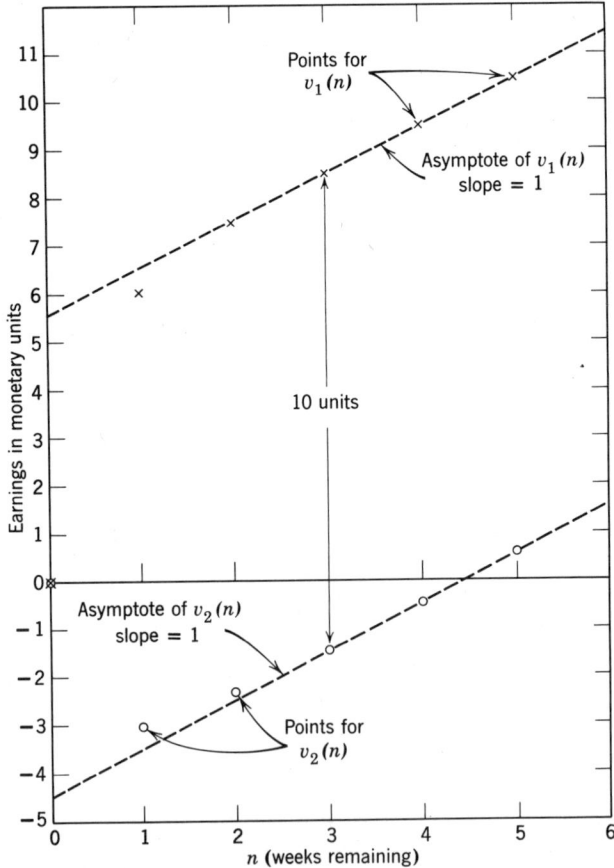

Fig. 2.1. Toymaker's problem; total expected reward in each state as a function of weeks remaining.

toy seems to be worth about 10 units more than having an unsuccessful one, as far as future return is concerned. Also, for large n, an additional week's operation brings about 1 unit of profit on the average. The behavior of $v_i(n)$ for large n is even more clear when the data of Table 2.1 are plotted as Fig. 2.1. The distance between the asymptotes to the value expressions is 10 units, whereas the slope of each asymptote is

1 unit. We shall be very much interested in the asymptotic behavior of total-earnings functions.

z-Transform Analysis of the Markov Process with Rewards

Let us analyze the Markov process with rewards by means of the z-transformation. The z-transform of the total-value vector $\mathbf{v}(n)$ will be called $\mathbf{v}(z)$ where $\mathbf{v}(z) = \sum_{n=0}^{\infty} \mathbf{v}(n)z^n$. Equation 2.5 may be written as

$$\mathbf{v}(n+1) = \mathbf{q} + \mathbf{P}\mathbf{v}(n) \qquad n = 0, 1, 2, \cdots \qquad (2.6)$$

If we take the z-transformation of this equation, we obtain

$$z^{-1}[\mathbf{v}(z) - \mathbf{v}(0)] = \frac{1}{1-z}\mathbf{q} + \mathbf{P}\mathbf{v}(z)$$

$$\mathbf{v}(z) - \mathbf{v}(0) = \frac{z}{1-z}\mathbf{q} + z\mathbf{P}\mathbf{v}(z)$$

$$(\mathbf{I} - z\mathbf{P})\mathbf{v}(z) = \frac{z}{1-z}\mathbf{q} + \mathbf{v}(0)$$

or

$$\mathbf{v}(z) = \frac{z}{1-z}(\mathbf{I} - z\mathbf{P})^{-1}\mathbf{q} + (\mathbf{I} - z\mathbf{P})^{-1}\mathbf{v}(0) \qquad (2.7)$$

Finding the transform $\mathbf{v}(z)$ requires the inverse of the matrix $(\mathbf{I} - z\mathbf{P})$, which also appeared in the solution for the state probabilities. This is not surprising since the presence of rewards does not affect the probabilistic structure of the process.

For the toymaker's problem, $\mathbf{v}(0)$ is identically zero, so that Eq. 2.7 reduces to

$$\mathbf{v}(z) = \frac{z}{1-z}(\mathbf{I} - z\mathbf{P})^{-1}\mathbf{q} \qquad (2.8)$$

For the toymaker process, the inverse matrix $(\mathbf{I} - z\mathbf{P})^{-1}$ was previously found to be

$$(\mathbf{I} - z\mathbf{P})^{-1} = \frac{1}{1-z}\begin{bmatrix} \frac{4}{9} & \frac{5}{9} \\ \frac{4}{9} & \frac{5}{9} \end{bmatrix} + \frac{1}{1-\frac{1}{10}z}\begin{bmatrix} \frac{5}{9} & -\frac{5}{9} \\ -\frac{4}{9} & \frac{4}{9} \end{bmatrix}$$

Thus

$$\frac{z}{1-z}(\mathbf{I}-z\mathbf{P})^{-1} = \frac{z}{(1-z)^2}\begin{bmatrix}\frac{4}{9} & \frac{5}{9}\\ \frac{4}{9} & \frac{5}{9}\end{bmatrix} + \frac{z}{(1-z)(1-\frac{1}{10}z)}\begin{bmatrix}\frac{5}{9} & -\frac{5}{9}\\ -\frac{4}{9} & \frac{4}{9}\end{bmatrix}$$

$$= \frac{z}{(1-z)^2}\begin{bmatrix}\frac{4}{9} & \frac{5}{9}\\ \frac{4}{9} & \frac{5}{9}\end{bmatrix} + \left(\frac{\frac{10}{9}}{1-z} + \frac{-\frac{10}{9}}{1-\frac{1}{10}z}\right)\begin{bmatrix}\frac{5}{9} & -\frac{5}{9}\\ -\frac{4}{9} & \frac{4}{9}\end{bmatrix}$$

Let the matrix $\mathbf{F}(n)$ be the inverse transform of $[z/(1-z)](\mathbf{I}-z\mathbf{P})^{-1}$. Then

$$\mathbf{F}(n) = n\begin{bmatrix}\frac{4}{9} & \frac{5}{9}\\ \frac{4}{9} & \frac{5}{9}\end{bmatrix} + \frac{10}{9}[1-(\tfrac{1}{10})^n]\begin{bmatrix}\frac{5}{9} & -\frac{5}{9}\\ -\frac{4}{9} & \frac{4}{9}\end{bmatrix}$$

The total-value vector $\mathbf{v}(n)$ is then $\mathbf{F}(n)\mathbf{q}$ by inverse transformation of Eq. 2.8, and, since $\mathbf{q} = \begin{bmatrix}6\\-3\end{bmatrix}$,

$$\mathbf{v}(n) = n\begin{bmatrix}1\\1\end{bmatrix} + \frac{10}{9}[1-(\tfrac{1}{10})^n]\begin{bmatrix}5\\-4\end{bmatrix}$$

In other words,

$$v_1(n) = n + \tfrac{50}{9}[1-(\tfrac{1}{10})^n] \qquad v_2(n) = n - \tfrac{40}{9}[1-(\tfrac{1}{10})^n] \quad (2.9)$$

We have thus found a closed-form expression for the total expected earnings starting in each state.

Equations 2.9 could be used to construct Table 2.1 or to draw Fig. 2.1. We see that, as n becomes very large, $v_1(n)$ takes the form $n + \tfrac{50}{9}$, whereas $v_2(n)$ takes the form $n - \tfrac{40}{9}$. The asymptotic relations

$$v_1(n) = n + \tfrac{50}{9}$$
$$v_2(n) = n - \tfrac{40}{9}$$

are the equations of the asymptotes shown in Fig. 2.1. Note that, for large n, both $v_1(n)$ and $v_2(n)$ have slope 1 and $v_1(n) - v_2(n) = 10$, as we saw previously. For large n, the slope of $v_1(n)$ or $v_2(n)$ is the average reward per transition, in this case 1. If the toymaker were many, many weeks from shutdown, he would expect to make 1 unit of return per week. We call the average reward per transition the "gain"; in this case the gain is 1 unit.

Asymptotic Behavior

What can be said in general about the total expected earnings of a

ASYMPTOTIC BEHAVIOR

process of long duration? To answer this question, let us return to Eq. 2.7:

$$\mathbf{v}(z) = \frac{z}{1-z}(\mathbf{I} - z\mathbf{P})^{-1}\mathbf{q} + (\mathbf{I} - z\mathbf{P})^{-1}\mathbf{v}(0) \tag{2.7}$$

It was shown in Chapter 1 that the inverse transform of $(\mathbf{I} - z\mathbf{P})^{-1}$ assumed the form $\mathbf{S} + \mathbf{T}(n)$. In this expression, $\mathbf{S}$ is a stochastic matrix whose ith row is the vector of limiting state probabilities if the system is started in the ith state, and $\mathbf{T}(n)$ is a set of differential matrices with geometrically decreasing coefficients. We shall write this relation in the form

$$(\mathbf{I} - z\mathbf{P})^{-1} = \frac{1}{1-z}\mathbf{S} + \mathscr{T}(z) \tag{2.10}$$

where $\mathscr{T}(z)$ is the z-transform of $\mathbf{T}(n)$. If we substitute Eq. 2.10 into Eq. 2.7, we obtain

$$\mathbf{v}(z) = \frac{z}{(1-z)^2}\mathbf{Sq} + \frac{z}{1-z}\mathscr{T}(z)\mathbf{q} + \frac{1}{1-z}\mathbf{Sv}(0) + \mathscr{T}(z)\mathbf{v}(0) \tag{2.11}$$

By inspection of this equation for $\mathbf{v}(z)$, we can identify the components of $\mathbf{v}(n)$. The term $[z/(1-z)^2]\mathbf{Sq}$ represents a ramp of magnitude $\mathbf{Sq}$. Partial-fraction expansion shows that the term $[z/(1-z)]\mathscr{T}(z)\mathbf{q}$ represents a step of magnitude $\mathscr{T}(1)\mathbf{q}$ plus geometric terms that tend to zero as n becomes very large. The quantity $[1/(1-z)]\mathbf{Sv}(0)$ is a step of magnitude $\mathbf{Sv}(0)$, whereas $\mathscr{T}(z)\mathbf{v}(0)$ represents geometric components that vanish when n is large. The asymptotic form that $\mathbf{v}(n)$ assumes for large n is thus

$$\mathbf{v}(n) = n\mathbf{Sq} + \mathscr{T}(1)\mathbf{q} + \mathbf{Sv}(0) \tag{2.12}$$

If a column vector $\mathbf{g}$ with components g_i is defined by $\mathbf{g} = \mathbf{Sq}$, then

$$\mathbf{v}(n) = n\mathbf{g} + \mathscr{T}(1)\mathbf{q} + \mathbf{Sv}(0) \tag{2.13}$$

The quantity g_i is equal to the sum of the immediate rewards q_j weighted by the limiting state probabilities that result if the system is started in the ith state, or

$$g_i = \sum_{j=1}^{N} s_{ij} q_j$$

It is also the average return per transition of the system if it is started in the ith state and allowed to make many transitions; we may call g_i the gain of the ith state. Equivalently, it is the slope of the asymptote of $v_i(n)$. Since all member states of the same recurrent chain have identical rows in the $\mathbf{S}$ matrix, such states all have the same gain.

If there is only one recurrent chain in the system so that it is completely ergodic, then all rows of **S** are the same and equal to the limiting state probability distribution for the process, **π**. It follows that in this case all states have the same gain, say g, and that

$$g = \sum_{i=1}^{N} \pi_i q_i \tag{2.14}$$

The column vector $\mathscr{T}(1)\mathbf{q} + \mathbf{Sv}(0)$ represents the intercepts at $n = 0$ of the asymptotes of $\mathbf{v}(n)$. These intercepts are jointly determined by the transient behavior of the process $\mathscr{T}(1)\mathbf{q}$ and by the boundary effect $\mathbf{Sv}(0)$. We shall denote by v_i the asymptotic intercepts of $v_i(n)$, so that for large n

$$v_i(n) = ng_i + v_i \qquad i = 1, 2, \cdots, N \tag{2.15}$$

The column vector with components v_i may be designated by **v** so that $\mathbf{v} = \mathscr{T}(1)\mathbf{q} + \mathbf{Sv}(0)$. Equations 2.15 then become

$$\mathbf{v}(n) = n\mathbf{g} + \mathbf{v} \qquad \text{for large } n \tag{2.16}$$

If the system is completely ergodic, then, of course, all $g_i = g$, and we may call g the gain of the process rather than the gain of a state, so that Eqs. 2.15 become

$$v_i(n) = ng + v_i \qquad i = 1, 2, \cdots, N \qquad \text{for large } n \tag{2.17}$$

By way of illustration for the toymaker's problem,

$$(\mathbf{I} - z\mathbf{P})^{-1} = \frac{1}{1-z}\begin{bmatrix} \frac{4}{9} & \frac{5}{9} \\ \frac{4}{9} & \frac{5}{9} \end{bmatrix} + \frac{1}{1-\frac{1}{10}z}\begin{bmatrix} \frac{5}{9} & -\frac{5}{9} \\ -\frac{4}{9} & \frac{4}{9} \end{bmatrix}$$

$$= \frac{1}{1-z}\mathbf{S} + \mathscr{T}(z)$$

so that

$$\mathbf{S} = \begin{bmatrix} \frac{4}{9} & \frac{5}{9} \\ \frac{4}{9} & \frac{5}{9} \end{bmatrix} \qquad \mathscr{T}(1) = \begin{bmatrix} \frac{50}{81} & -\frac{50}{81} \\ -\frac{40}{81} & \frac{40}{81} \end{bmatrix}$$

Since

$$\mathbf{q} = \begin{bmatrix} 6 \\ -3 \end{bmatrix} \qquad \mathbf{g} = \mathbf{Sq} = \begin{bmatrix} 1 \\ 1 \end{bmatrix}$$

By assumption, $\mathbf{v}(0) = 0$; then

$$\mathbf{v} = \mathscr{T}(1)\mathbf{q} = \begin{bmatrix} \frac{50}{9} \\ -\frac{40}{9} \end{bmatrix}$$

ASYMPTOTIC BEHAVIOR

Therefore, from Eqs. 2.15,

$$v_1(n) = n + \tfrac{50}{9} \qquad v_2(n) = n - \tfrac{40}{9} \qquad \text{for large } n$$

as we found before.

We have now discussed the analysis of Markov processes with rewards. Special attention has been paid to the asymptotic behavior of the total expected reward function, for reasons that will become clear in later chapters.

3

The Solution of the Sequential Decision Process by Value Iteration

The discussion of Markov processes with rewards has been the means to an end. This end is the analysis of decisions in sequential processes that are Markovian in nature. This chapter will describe the type of process under consideration and will show a method of solution based on recurrence relations.

Introduction of Alternatives

The toymaker's problem that we have been discussing may be described as follows. If the toymaker is in state 1 (successful toy), he makes transitions to state 1 and state 2 (unsuccessful toy) according to a probability distribution $[p_{1j}] = [0.5\ \ 0.5]$ and earns rewards according to the reward distribution $[r_{1j}] = [9\ \ 3]$. If the toymaker is in state 2, the pertinent probability and reward distributions are $[p_{2j}] = [0.4\ \ 0.6]$ and $[r_{2j}] = [3\ \ -7]$. This process has been analyzed in detail; we know how to calculate the expected earnings for any number of transitions before the toymaker goes out of business.

Suppose now that the toymaker has other courses of action open to him that will change the probabilities and rewards governing the process. For example, when the toymaker has a successful toy, he may use advertising to decrease the chance that the toy will fall from favor. However, because of the advertising cost, the profits to be expected per week will generally be lower. To be specific, suppose that the probability distribution for transitions from state 1 will be $[p_{1j}] = [0.8\ \ 0.2]$ when advertising is employed, and that the

INTRODUCTION OF ALTERNATIVES

corresponding reward distribution will be $[r_{1j}] = [4 \quad 4]$. The toymaker now has two alternatives when he is in state 1: He may use no advertising or he may advertise. We shall call these alternatives 1 and 2, respectively. Each alternative has its associated reward and probability distributions for transitions out of state 1. We shall use a superscript k to indicate the alternatives in a state. Thus, for alternative 1 in state 1, $[p_{1j}{}^1] = [0.5 \quad 0.5]$, $[r_{1j}{}^1] = [9 \quad 3]$; and for alternative 2 in state 1, $[p_{1j}{}^2] = [0.8 \quad 0.2]$, $[r_{1j}{}^2] = [4 \quad 4]$.

There may also be alternatives in state 2 of the system (the company has an unsuccessful toy). Increased research expenditures may increase the probability of obtaining a successful toy, but they will also increase the cost of being in state 2. Under the original alternative in state 2, which we may call alternative 1 and interpret as a limited research alternative, the transition probability distribution was $[p_{2j}] = [0.4 \quad 0.6]$, and the reward distribution was $[r_{2j}] = [3 \quad -7]$. Under the research alternative, alternative 2, the probability and reward distribution might be $[p_{2j}] = [0.7 \quad 0.3]$ and $[r_{2j}] = [1 \quad -19]$. Thus, for alternative 1 in state 2,

$$[p_{2j}{}^1] = [0.4 \quad 0.6] \qquad [r_{2j}{}^1] = [3 \quad -7]$$

and for alternative 2 in state 2,

$$[p_{2j}{}^2] = [0.7 \quad 0.3] \qquad [r_{2j}{}^2] = [1 \quad -19]$$

The concept of alternative for an N-state system is presented graphically in Fig. 3.1. In this diagram, two alternatives have been

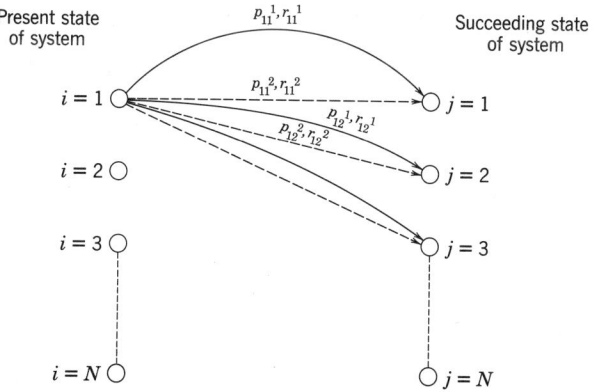

Fig. 3.1. Diagram of states and alternatives.

allowed in the first state. If we pick alternative 1 ($k = 1$), then the transition from state 1 to state 1 will be governed by the probability

p_{11}^1, the transition from state 1 to state 2 will be governed by p_{12}^1, from 1 to 3 by p_{13}^1, and so on. The rewards associated with these transitions are r_{11}^1, r_{12}^1, r_{13}^1, and so on. If the second alternative in state 1 is chosen ($k = 2$), then p_{11}^2, p_{12}^2, p_{13}^2, $\cdots$, p_{1N}^2 and r_{11}^2, r_{12}^2, r_{13}^2, $\cdots$, r_{1N}^2, and so on, would be the pertinent probabilities and rewards, respectively. In Fig. 3.1 we see that, if alternative 1 in state 1 is selected, we make transitions according to the solid lines; if alternative 2 is chosen, transitions are made according to the dashed lines. The number of alternatives in any state must be finite, but the number of alternatives in each state may be different from the numbers in other states.

The Toymaker's Problem Solved by Value Iteration

The alternatives for the toymaker are presented in Table 3.1. The quantity q_i^k is the expected reward from a single transition from state i under alternative k. Thus, $q_i^k = \sum_{j=1}^{N} p_{ij}^k r_{ij}^k$.

Table 3.1. THE TOYMAKER'S SEQUENTIAL DECISION PROBLEM

State i	Alternative k	Transition Probabilities		Rewards		Expected Immediate Reward q_i^k
		p_{i1}^k	p_{i2}^k	r_{i1}^k	r_{i2}^k	
1 (Successful toy)	1 (No advertising)	0.5	0.5	9	3	6
	2 (Advertising)	0.8	0.2	4	4	4
2 (Unsuccessful toy)	1 (No research)	0.4	0.6	3	-7	-3
	2 (Research)	0.7	0.3	1	-19	-5

Suppose that the toymaker has n weeks remaining before his business will close down. We shall call n the number of stages remaining in the process. The toymaker would like to know as a function of n and his present state what alternative he should use for the next transition (week) in order to maximize the total earnings of his business over the n-week period.

We shall define $d_i(n)$ as the number of the alternative in the ith state that will be used at stage n. We call $d_i(n)$ the "decision" in state i at the nth stage. When $d_i(n)$ has been specified for all i and all n, a "policy" has been determined. The optimal policy is the one that maximizes total expected return for each i and n.

To analyze this problem, let us redefine $v_i(n)$ as the total expected

TOYMAKER'S PROBLEM SOLVED BY VALUE ITERATION

return in n stages starting from state i *if an optimal policy is followed*. It follows that for any n

$$v_i(n+1) = \max_k \sum_{j=1}^{N} p_{ij}{}^k [r_{ij}{}^k + v_j(n)] \qquad n = 0, 1, 2, \cdots \quad (3.1)$$

Suppose that we have decided which alternatives to follow at stages n, $n-1, \cdots, 1$ in such a way that we have maximized $v_j(n)$ for $j = 1, 2, \cdots, N$. We are at stage $n+1$ and are seeking the alternative we should follow in the ith state in order to make $v_i(n+1)$ as large as possible; this is $d_i(n+1)$. If we used alternative k in the ith state, then our expected return for $n+1$ stages would be

$$\sum_{j=1}^{N} p_{ij}{}^k [r_{ij}{}^k + v_j(n)] \qquad (3.2)$$

by the argument of Chapter 2. We are seeking the alternative in the ith state that will maximize Expression 3.2. For this alternative, $v_i(n+1)$ will be equal to Expression 3.2; thus we have derived Eq. 3.1,* which we may call the value iteration equation. Equation 3.1 may be written in terms of the expected immediate rewards from each alternative in the form

$$v_i(n+1) = \max_k \left[q_i{}^k + \sum_{j=1}^{N} p_{ij}{}^k v_j(n) \right] \qquad (3.3)$$

The use of the recursive relation (Eq. 3.3) will tell the toymaker which alternative to use in each state at each stage and will also provide him with his expected future earnings at each stage of the process. To apply this relation, we must specify $v_j(0)$ the boundary condition for the process. We shall assign the value 0 to both $v_1(0)$ and $v_2(0)$, as we did in Chapter 2. Now Eq. 3.3 will be used to solve the toymaker's problem as presented in Table 3.1. The results are shown in Table 3.2.

Table 3.2. TOYMAKER'S PROBLEM SOLVED BY VALUE ITERATION

$n =$	0	1	2	3	4	...
$v_1(n)$	0	6	8.2	10.22	12.222	...
$v_2(n)$	0	−3	−1.7	0.23	2.223	...
$d_1(n)$	—	1	2	2	2	...
$d_2(n)$	—	1	2	2	2	...

The calculation will be illustrated by finding the alternatives and

* Equation 3.1 is the application of the "Principle of Optimality" of dynamic programming to the Markovian decision process; this and other applications are discussed by Bellman.[1]

rewards at the first stage. Since $\mathbf{v}(0) = 0$, $v_1(1) = \max_k q_1{}^k$. The alternative to be used in state 1 at the first stage is that with the largest expected immediate reward. Since $q_1{}^1 = 6$ and $q_1{}^2 = 4$, the first alternative in state 1 is the better one to use at the first stage, and $v_1(1) = 6$. Similarly, $v_2(1) = \max_k q_2{}^k$, and, since, $q_2{}^1 = -3$, and $q_2{}^2 = -5$, the first alternative in state 2 is the better alternative and $v_2(1) = -3$. Having now calculated $v_i(1)$ for all states, we may again use Eq. 3.3 to calculate $v_i(2)$ and to determine the alternatives to be used at the second stage. The process may be continued for as many n as we care to calculate.

Suppose that the toymaker has three weeks remaining and that he is in state 1. Then we see from Table 3.2 that he expects to make 10.22 units of reward in this period of time, $v_1(3) = 10.22$, and that he should advertise during the coming week, $d_1(3) = 2$. We may similarly interpret any other situation in which the toymaker may find himself.

Note that for $n = 2$, 3, and 4, the second alternative in each state is to be preferred. This means that the toymaker is better advised to advertise and to carry on research in spite of the costs of these activities. The changes produced in the transition probabilities more than make up for the additional cost. It has been shown[1] that the iteration process (Eq. 3.3) will converge on a best alternative for each state as n becomes very large. For this problem the convergence seems to have taken place at $n = 2$, and the second alternative in each state has been chosen. However, in many problems it is difficult to tell when convergence has been obtained.

Evaluation of the Value-Iteration Approach

The method that has just been described for the solution of the sequential process may be called the value-iteration method because the $v_i(n)$ or "values" are determined iteratively. This method has some important limitations. It must be clear to the reader that not many enterprises or processes operate with the specter of termination so imminent. For the most part, systems operate on an indefinite basis with no clearly defined end point. It does not seem efficient to have to iterate $v_i(n)$ for $n = 1, 2, 3$, and so forth, until we have a sufficiently large n that termination is very remote. We would much rather have a method that directed itself to the problem of analyzing processes of indefinite duration, processes that will make many transitions before termination.

Such a technique has been developed; it will be presented in the next chapter. Recall that, even if we were patient enough to solve the long-duration process by value iteration, the convergence on the best alternative in each state is asymptotic and difficult to measure analytically. The method to be presented circumvents this difficulty.

Even though the value-iteration method is not particularly suited to long-duration processes, it is relevant to those systems that face termination in a relatively short time. However, it is important to recognize that often the process need not have many stages before a long-duration analysis becomes meaningful.

4

The Policy-Iteration Method for the Solution of Sequential Decision Processes

Consider a completely ergodic N-state Markov process described by a transition-probability matrix **P** and a reward matrix **R**. Suppose that the process is allowed to make transitions for a very, very long time and that we are interested in the earnings of the process. The total expected earnings depend upon the total number of transitions that the system undergoes, so that this quantity grows without limit as the number of transitions increases. A more useful quantity is the average earnings of the process per unit time. It was shown in Chapter 2 that this quantity is meaningful if the process is allowed to make many transitions; it was called the gain of the process.

Since the system is completely ergodic, the limiting state probabilities π_i are independent of the starting state, and the gain g of the system is

$$g = \sum_{i=1}^{N} \pi_i q_i \qquad (2.14)$$

where q_i is the expected immediate return in state i defined by Eq. 2.3.

Every completely ergodic Markov process with rewards will have a gain given by Eq. 2.14. If we have several such processes and we should like to know which would be most profitable on a long-term basis, we could find the gain of each and then select the one with highest gain.

The sequential decision process of Chapter 3 requires consideration of many possible processes because the alternatives in each state may be selected independently. By way of illustration, consider the

THE POLICY-ITERATION METHOD

three-dimensional array of Fig. 4.1, which presents in graphical form the states and alternatives.

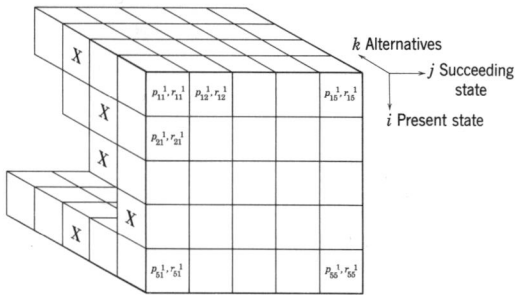

Fig. 4.1. A possible five-state problem.

The array as drawn illustrates a five-state problem that has four alternatives in the first state, three in the second, two in the third, one in the fourth, and five in the fifth. Entered on the face of the array are the parameters for the first alternative in each state, the second row in depth of the array contains the parameters for the second alternative in each state, and so forth. An X indicates that we have chosen a particular alternative in a state with a probability and reward distribution that will govern the behavior of the system at any time that it enters that state. The alternative thus selected is called the "decision" for that state; it is no longer a function of n. The set of X's or the set of decisions for all states is called a "policy." Selection of a policy thus determines the Markov process with rewards that will describe the operations of the system. The policy indicated in the diagram requires that the probability and reward matrices for the system be composed of the first alternative in state 4, the second alternative in states 2 and 3, and the third alternative in states 1 and 5. It is possible to describe the policy by a decision vector $\mathbf{d}$ whose elements represent the number of the alternative selected in each state. In this case

$$\mathbf{d} = \begin{bmatrix} 3 \\ 2 \\ 2 \\ 1 \\ 3 \end{bmatrix}$$

An optimal policy is defined as a policy that maximizes the gain, or average return per transition.* In the five-state problem diagrammed in Fig. 4.1, there are $4 \times 3 \times 2 \times 1 \times 5 = 120$ different

---

* We shall assume for the moment that all policies produce completely ergodic Markov processes. This assumption will be relaxed in Chapter 6.

policies. It is conceivable that we could find the gain for each of these policies in order to find the policy with the largest gain. However feasible this may be for 120 policies, it becomes unfeasible for very large problems. For example, a problem with 50 states and 50 alternatives in each state contains $50^{50} (\approx 10^{85})$ policies.

The policy-iteration method that will be described will find the optimal policy in a small number of iterations. It is composed of two parts, the value-determination operation and the policy-improvement routine. We shall first discuss the value-determination operation.

The Value-Determination Operation

Suppose that we are operating the system under a given policy so that we have specified a given Markov process with rewards. If this process were to be allowed to operate for n stages or transitions, we could define $v_i(n)$ as the total expected reward that the system will earn in n moves if it starts from state i *under the given policy*.

The quantity $v_i(n)$ must obey the recurrence relation (Eq. 2.4) derived in Chapter 2:

$$v_i(n) = q_i + \sum_{j=1}^{N} p_{ij} v_j(n-1) \qquad i = 1, 2, \cdots, N \qquad n = 1, 2, 3, \cdots \quad (2.4)$$

There is no need for a superscript k to appear in this equation because the establishment of a policy has defined the probability and reward matrices that describe the system.

It was shown in Chapter 2 that for completely ergodic Markov processes $v_i(n)$ had the asymptotic form

$$v_i(n) = ng + v_i \qquad i = 1, 2, \cdots, N \qquad \text{for large } n \quad (2.17)$$

In this chapter we are concerned only with systems that have a very, very large number of stages. We are then justified in using Eq. 2.17 in Eq. 2.4. We obtain the equations

$$ng + v_i = q_i + \sum_{j=1}^{N} p_{ij}[(n-1)g + v_j] \qquad i = 1, 2, \cdots, N$$

$$ng + v_i = q_i + (n-1)g \sum_{j=1}^{N} p_{ij} + \sum_{j=1}^{N} p_{ij} v_j$$

Since $\sum_{j=1}^{N} p_{ij} = 1$, these equations become

$$g + v_i = q_i + \sum_{j=1}^{N} p_{ij} v_j \qquad i = 1, 2, \cdots, N \quad (4.1)$$

VALUE-DETERMINATION OPERATION

We have now obtained a set of N linear simultaneous equations that relate the quantities v_i and g to the probability and reward structure of the process. However, a count of unknowns reveals N v_i and 1 g to be determined, a total of $N + 1$ unknowns. The nature of this difficulty may be understood if we examine the result of adding a constant a to all v_i in Eqs. 4.1. These equations become

$$g + v_i + a = q_i + \sum_{j=1}^{N} p_{ij}(v_j + a)$$

or

$$g + v_i = q_i + \sum_{j=1}^{N} p_{ij} v_j$$

The original equations have been obtained once more, so that the absolute value of the v_i cannot be determined by the equations. However, if we set one of the v_i equal to zero, perhaps v_N, then only N unknowns are present, and the Eqs. 4.1 may be solved for g and the remaining v_i. Notice that the v_i so obtained will not be those defined by Eq. 2.17 but will differ from them by a constant amount. Nevertheless, because the true values of the v_i contain a constant term

$$\sum_{i=1}^{N} \pi_i v_i(0)$$

as shown in Eq. 2.13, they have no real significance in processes that continue for a very large number of transitions. The v_i produced by the solution of Eqs. 4.1 with $v_N = 0$ will be sufficient for our purposes; they will be called the relative values of the policy.

The relative values may be given a physical interpretation. Consider the first two states, 1 and 2. For any large n, Eq. 2.17 yields

$$v_1(n) = ng + v_1 \qquad v_2(n) = ng + v_2$$

The difference $v_1(n) - v_2(n) = v_1 - v_2$ for any large n; it is equal to the increase in the long-run expected earnings of the system caused by starting in state 1 rather than state 2. Since the difference $v_1 - v_2$ is independent of any absolute level, the relative values may be used to find the difference. In other words, the difference in the relative values of the two states $v_1 - v_2$ is equal to the amount that a rational man would be just willing to pay in order to start his transitions from state 1 rather than state 2 if he is going to operate the system for many, many transitions. We shall exploit this interpretation of the relative values in the examples of Chapter 5.

If Eqs. 4.1 are multiplied by π_i, the limiting state probability of the ith state, and then summed over i, we obtain

$$g \sum_{i=1}^{N} \pi_i + \sum_{i=1}^{N} \pi_i v_i = \sum_{i=1}^{N} \pi_i q_i + \sum_{j=1}^{N} \sum_{i=1}^{N} \pi_i p_{ij} v_j$$

The basic equations (Eqs. 1.5 and 1.6) show that this expression is equivalent to Eq. 2.14:

$$g = \sum_{i=1}^{N} \pi_i q_i \qquad (2.14)$$

A relevant question at this point is this: If we are seeking only the gain of the given policy, why did we not use Eq. 2.14 rather than Eq. 4.1? As a matter of fact, why are we bothering to find such things as relative values at all? The answer is first, that although Eq. 2.14 does find the gain of the process it does not inform us about how to find a better policy. We shall see that the relative values hold the key to finding better and better policies and ultimately the best policy.

A second part of the answer is that the amount of computational effort required to solve Eqs. 4.1 for the gain and relative values is about the same as that required to find the limiting state probabilities using Eqs. 1.5 and 1.6, because both computations require the solution of N linear simultaneous equations. From the point of view of finding the gain, Eqs. 2.14 and 4.1 are a standoff; however, Eqs. 4.1 are to be preferred because they yield the relative values that will be shown to be necessary for policy improvement.

From the point of view of computation, it is interesting to note that we have considerable freedom in scaling our rewards because of the linearity of Eqs. 4.1. If the rewards r_{ij} of a process with gain g and relative values v_i are modified by a linear transformation to yield new rewards r_{ij}' in the sense $r_{ij}' = ar_{ij} + b$, then since

$$q_i = \sum_{j=1}^{N} p_{ij} r_{ij}$$

the new expected immediate rewards q_i' will be $q_i' = aq_i + b$, so that the q_i are subjected to the same transformation. Equations 4.1 become

$$g + v_i = \frac{q_i' - b}{a} + \sum_{j=1}^{N} p_{ij} v_j \qquad i = 1, 2, \cdots, N$$

or

$$(ag + b) + (av_i) = q_i' + \sum_{j=1}^{N} p_{ij}(av_j)$$

and

$$g' + v_i' = q_i' + \sum_{j=1}^{N} p_{ij} v_j'$$

The gain g' of the process with transformed rewards is thus $ag + b$, whereas the values v_i' of this process will equal av_i. The effect of changes in the units of measurement and in the absolute level of the reward system upon the gain and relative values is easily calculated. Thus we could normalize all rewards to be between 0 and 1, solve the entire sequential decision process, and then use the inverse of our original transformation to return the gain and relative values to their original levels.

We have now shown that for a given policy we can find the gain and relative values of that policy by solving the N linear simultaneous equations (Eqs. 4.1) with $v_N = 0$. We shall now show how the relative values may be used to find a policy that has higher gain than the original policy.

The Policy-Improvement Routine

In Chapter 3 we found that if we had an optimal policy up to stage n we could find the best alternative in the ith state at stage $n + 1$ by maximizing

$$q_i^k + \sum_{j=1}^{N} p_{ij}^k v_j(n) \qquad (4.2)$$

over all alternatives in the ith state. For large n, we could substitute Eq. 2.17 to obtain

$$q_i^k + \sum_{j=1}^{N} p_{ij}^k (ng + v_j) \qquad (4.3)$$

as the test quantity to be maximized in each state. Since

$$\sum_{j=1}^{N} p_{ij}^k = 1$$

the contribution of ng and any additive constant in the v_j becomes a test-quantity component that is independent of k. Thus, when we are making our decision in state i, we can maximize

$$q_i^k + \sum_{j=1}^{N} p_{ij}^k v_j \qquad (4.4)$$

with respect to the alternatives in the ith state. Furthermore, we can use the relative values (as given by Eqs. 4.1) for the policy that was used up to stage n.

The policy-improvement routine may be summarized as follows: For each state i, find the alternative k that maximizes the test quantity

$$q_i^k + \sum_{j=1}^{N} p_{ij}^k v_j$$

using the relative values determined under the old policy. This alternative k now becomes d_i, the decision in the ith state. A new policy has been determined when this procedure has been performed for every state.

We have now, by somewhat heuristic means, described a method for finding a policy that is an improvement over our original policy. We shall soon prove that the new policy will have a higher gain than the old policy. First, however, we shall show how the value-determination operation and the policy-improvement routine are combined in an iteration cycle whose goal is the discovery of the policy that has highest gain among all possible policies.

The Iteration Cycle

The basic iteration cycle may be diagrammed as shown in Figure 4.2.

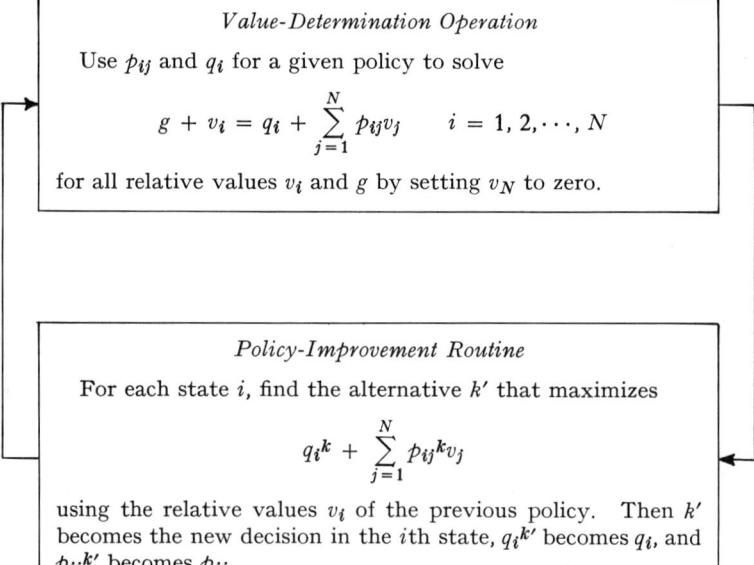

Fig. 4.2. The iteration cycle.

The upper box, the value-determination operation, yields the g and v_i corresponding to a given choice of q_i and p_{ij}. The lower box yields the p_{ij} and q_i that increase the gain for a given set of v_i. In other words, the value-determination operation yields values as a function of policy, whereas the policy-improvement routine yields the policy as a function of the values.

We may enter the iteration cycle in either box. If the value-determination operation is chosen as the entrance point, an initial policy must be selected. If the cycle is to start in the policy-improvement routine, then a starting set of values is necessary. If there is no *a priori* reason for selecting a particular initial policy or for choosing a certain starting set of values, then it is often convenient to start the process in the policy-improvement routine with all $v_i = 0$. In this case, the policy-improvement routine will select a policy as follows:

For each i, it will find the alternative k' that maximizes q_i^k and then set $d_i = k'$.

This starting procedure will consequently cause the policy-improvement routine to select as an initial policy the one that maximizes the expected immediate reward in each state. The iteration will then proceed to the value-determination operation with this policy, and the iteration cycle will begin. The selection of an initial policy that maximizes expected immediate reward is quite satisfactory in the majority of cases.

At this point it would be wise to say a few words about how to stop the iteration cycle once it has done its job. The rule is quite simple: The optimal policy has been reached (g is maximized) when the policies on two successive iterations are identical. In order to prevent the policy-improvement routine from quibbling over equally good alternatives in a particular state, it is only necessary to require that the old d_i be left unchanged if the test quantity for that d_i is as large as that of any other alternative in the new policy determination.

In summary, the policy-iteration method just described has the following properties:

1. The solution of the sequential decision process is reduced to solving sets of linear simultaneous equations and subsequent comparisons.

2. Each succeeding policy found in the iteration cycle has a higher gain than the previous one.

3. The iteration cycle will terminate on the policy that has largest gain attainable within the realm of the problem; it will usually find this policy in a small number of iterations.

Before proving properties 2 and 3, let us see the policy-iteration method in action by applying it to the toymaker's problem.

The Toymaker's Problem

The data for the toymaker's problem were presented in Table 3.1.

There are two states and two alternatives in each state, so that there are four possible policies for the toymaker, each with associated probabilities and rewards. He would like to know which of these four policies he should follow into the indefinite future to make his average earnings per week as large as possible.

Let us suppose that we have no *a priori* knowledge about which policy is best. Then if we set $v_1 = v_2 = 0$ and enter the policy-improvement routine, it will select as an initial policy the one that maximizes expected immediate reward in each state. For the toymaker, this policy consists of selection of alternative 1 in both states 1 and 2. For this policy

$$\mathbf{d} = \begin{bmatrix} 1 \\ 1 \end{bmatrix} \qquad \mathbf{P} = \begin{bmatrix} 0.5 & 0.5 \\ 0.4 & 0.6 \end{bmatrix} \qquad \mathbf{q} = \begin{bmatrix} 6 \\ -3 \end{bmatrix}$$

We are now ready to begin the value-determination operation that will evaluate our initial policy. From Eqs. 4.1,

$$g + v_1 = 6 + 0.5v_1 + 0.5v_2 \qquad g + v_2 = -3 + 0.4v_1 + 0.6v_2$$

Setting $v_2 = 0$ and solving these equations, we obtain

$$g = 1 \qquad v_1 = 10 \qquad v_2 = 0$$

(Recall that by use of a different method the gain of 1 was obtained earlier for this policy.) We are now ready to enter the policy-improvement routine as shown in Table 4.1.

Table 4.1. TOYMAKER POLICY-IMPROVEMENT ROUTINE

State i	Alternative k	Test Quantity $q_i^k + \sum_{j=1}^{N} p_{ij}^k v_j$
1	1	$6 + 0.5(10) + 0.5(0) = 11$
	2	$4 + 0.8(10) + 0.2(0) = 12 \leftarrow$
2	1	$-3 + 0.4(10) + 0.6(0) = 1$
	2	$-5 + 0.7(10) + 0.3(0) = 2 \leftarrow$

The policy-improvement routine reveals that the second alternative in each state produces a higher value of the test quantity

$$q_i^k + \sum_{j=1}^{N} p_{ij}^k v_j$$

than does the first alternative. Thus the policy composed of the second alternative in each state will have a higher gain than our original policy.

THE TOYMAKER'S PROBLEM

However, we must continue our procedure because we are not yet sure that the new policy is the best we can find. For this policy,

$$\mathbf{d} = \begin{bmatrix} 2 \\ 2 \end{bmatrix} \qquad \mathbf{P} = \begin{bmatrix} 0.8 & 0.2 \\ 0.7 & 0.3 \end{bmatrix} \qquad \mathbf{q} = \begin{bmatrix} 4 \\ -5 \end{bmatrix}$$

Equations 4.1 for this case become

$$g + v_1 = 4 + 0.8v_1 + 0.2v_2$$
$$g + v_2 = -5 + 0.7v_1 + 0.3v_2$$

With $v_2 = 0$, the results of the value-determination operation are

$$g = 2 \qquad v_1 = 10 \qquad v_2 = 0$$

The gain of the policy $\mathbf{d} = \begin{bmatrix} 2 \\ 2 \end{bmatrix}$ is thus twice that of the original policy. We must now enter the policy-improvement routine again, but, since the relative values are coincidentally the same as those for the previous iteration, the calculations in Table 4.1 are merely repeated. The policy $\mathbf{d} = \begin{bmatrix} 2 \\ 2 \end{bmatrix}$ is found once more, and, since we have found the same policy twice in succession, we have found the optimal policy. The toymaker should follow the second alternative in each state. If he does, he will earn 2 units per week on the average, and this will be a higher average earning rate than that offered by any other policy. The reader should verify, for example, that both policy $\mathbf{d} = \begin{bmatrix} 1 \\ 2 \end{bmatrix}$ and policy $\mathbf{d} = \begin{bmatrix} 2 \\ 1 \end{bmatrix}$ have inferior gains.

For the optimal policy, $v_1 = 10$, $v_2 = 0$, so that $v_1 - v_2 = 10$. This means that, even when the toymaker is following the optimal policy by using advertising and research, he is willing to pay up to 10 units to an outside inventor for a successful toy at any time that he does not have one. The relative values of the optimal policy may be used in this way to aid the toymaker in making "one-of-a-kind" decisions about whether to buy rights to a successful toy when business is bad.

The optimal policy for the toymaker was found by value iteration in Chapter 3. The similarities and differences of the two methods should now be clear. Note how the policy-iteration method stopped of its own accord when it achieved policy convergence; there is no comparable behavior in the value-iteration method. The policy-iteration method has a simplicity of form and interpretation that makes it very desirable from a computational point of view. However, we must always bear

A Proof of the Properties of the Policy-Iteration Method

Suppose that we have evaluated a policy A for the operation of the system and that the policy-improvement routine has produced a policy B that is different from A. Then if we use superscripts A and B to indicate the quantities relevant to policies A and B, we seek to prove that $g^B > g^A$.

It follows from the definition of the policy-improvement routine that, since B was chosen over A,

$$q_i^B + \sum_{j=1}^{N} p_{ij}^B v_j^A \geq q_i^A + \sum_{j=1}^{N} p_{ij}^A v_j^A \qquad i = 1, 2, \cdots, N \qquad (4.5)$$

Let

$$\gamma_i = q_i^B + \sum_{j=1}^{N} p_{ij}^B v_j^A - q_i^A - \sum_{j=1}^{N} p_{ij}^A v_j^A \qquad (4.6)$$

so that $\gamma_i \geq 0$. The quantity γ_i is the improvement in the test quantity that the policy-improvement routine was able to achieve in the ith state. For policies A and B individually, we have from Eqs. 4.1

$$g^B + v_i^B = q_i^B + \sum_{j=1}^{N} p_{ij}^B v_j^B \qquad i = 1, 2, \cdots, N \qquad (4.7)$$

$$g^A + v_i^A = q_i^A + \sum_{j=1}^{N} p_{ij}^A v_j^A \qquad i = 1, 2, \cdots, N \qquad (4.8)$$

If Eq. 4.8 is subtracted from Eq. 4.7, then the result is

$$g^B - g^A + v_i^B - v_i^A = q_i^B - q_i^A + \sum_{j=1}^{N} p_{ij}^B v_j^B - \sum_{j=1}^{N} p_{ij}^A v_j^A \qquad (4.9)$$

If Eq. 4.6 is solved for $q_i^B - q_i^A$ and this result is substituted into Eq. 4.9, then we have

$$g^B - g^A + v_i^B - v_i^A = \gamma_i - \sum_{j=1}^{N} p_{ij}^B v_j^A + \sum_{j=1}^{N} p_{ij}^A v_j^A$$
$$+ \sum_{j=1}^{N} p_{ij}^B v_j^B - \sum_{j=1}^{N} p_{ij}^A v_j^A$$

or

$$g^B - g^A + v_i^B - v_i^A = \gamma_i + \sum_{j=1}^{N} p_{ij}^B (v_j^B - v_j^A) \qquad (4.10)$$

A PROOF OF THE POLICY-ITERATION METHOD

Let $g^\Delta = g^B - g^A$ and $v_i^\Delta = v_i^B - v_i^A$. Then Eq. 4.10 becomes

$$g^\Delta + v_i^\Delta = \gamma_i + \sum_{j=1}^{N} p_{ij}{}^B v_j{}^\Delta \qquad i = 1, 2, \cdots, N \qquad (4.11)$$

Equations 4.11 are identical in form to Eqs. 4.1 except that they are written in terms of differences rather than in terms of absolute quantities. Just as the solution for g obtained from Eqs. 4.1 is

$$g = \sum_{i=1}^{N} \pi_i q_i$$

so the solution for g^Δ in Eqs. 4.11 is

$$g^\Delta = \sum_{i=1}^{N} \pi_i{}^B \gamma_i \qquad (4.12)$$

where $\pi_i{}^B$ is the limiting state probability of state i under policy B.

Since all $\pi_i{}^B \geqslant 0$ and all $\gamma_i \geqslant 0$, therefore, $g^\Delta \geqslant 0$. In particular, g^B will be greater than g^A if an improvement in the test quantity can be made in any state that will be recurrent under policy B. We see from Eq. 4.12 that the increases in gain caused by improvements in each recurrent state of the new policy are additive. Even if we performed our policy improvement on only one state and left other decisions unchanged, the gain of the system would increase if this state is recurrent under the new policy.

We shall now show that it is impossible for a better policy to exist and not be found at some time by the policy-improvement routine. Assume that, for two policies A and B, $g^B > g^A$, but the policy-improvement routine has converged on policy A. Then in all states, $\gamma_i \leqslant 0$, where γ_i is defined by Eq. 4.6. Since $\pi_i{}^B \geqslant 0$ for all i, Eq. 4.12 holds that $g^B - g^A \leqslant 0$. But $g^B > g^A$ by assumption, so that a contradiction has been reached. It is thus impossible for a superior policy to remain undiscovered.

The following chapter will present further examples of the policy-iteration method that show how it may be applied to a variety of problems.

5

Use of the Policy-Iteration Method in Problems of Taxicab Operation, Baseball, and Automobile Replacement

An Example—Taxicab Operation

Consider the problem of a taxicab driver whose territory encompasses three towns, A, B, and C. If he is in town A, he has three alternatives:

1. He can cruise in the hope of picking up a passenger by being hailed.
2. He can drive to the nearest cab stand and wait in line.
3. He can pull over and wait for a radio call.

If he is in town C, he has the same three alternatives, but if he is in town B, the last alternative is not present because there is no radio cab service in that town. For a given town and given alternative, there is a probability that the next trip will go to each of the towns A, B, and C and a corresponding reward in monetary units associated with each such trip. This reward represents the income from the trip after all necessary expenses have been deducted. For example, in the case of alternatives 1 and 2, the cost of cruising and of driving to the nearest stand must be included in calculating the rewards. The probabilities of transition and the rewards depend upon the alternative because different customer population will be encountered under each alternative.

If we identify being in towns A, B, and C with states 1, 2, and 3, respectively, then we have Table 5.1.

TAXICAB OPERATION

Table 5.1. Data for Taxicab Problem

State	Alternative	Probability p_{ij}^{k}			Reward r_{ij}^{k}			Expected Immediate Reward $q_i^k = \sum_{j=1}^{N} p_{ij}^{k} r_{ij}^{k}$
i	k	$j=1$	2	3	$j=1$	2	3	
1	1	$\frac{1}{2}$	$\frac{1}{4}$	$\frac{1}{4}$	10	4	8	8
	2	$\frac{1}{16}$	$\frac{3}{4}$	$\frac{3}{16}$	8	2	4	2.75
	3	$\frac{1}{4}$	$\frac{1}{8}$	$\frac{5}{8}$	4	6	4	4.25
2	1	$\frac{1}{2}$	0	$\frac{1}{2}$	14	0	18	16
	2	$\frac{1}{16}$	$\frac{7}{8}$	$\frac{1}{16}$	8	16	8	15
3	1	$\frac{1}{4}$	$\frac{1}{4}$	$\frac{1}{2}$	10	2	8	7
	2	$\frac{1}{8}$	$\frac{3}{4}$	$\frac{1}{8}$	6	4	2	4
	3	$\frac{3}{4}$	$\frac{1}{16}$	$\frac{3}{16}$	4	0	8	4.5

The reward is measured in some arbitrary monetary unit; the numbers in Table 5.1 are chosen more for ease of calculation than for any other reason.

In order to start the decision-making process, suppose that we make v_1, v_2, and $v_3 = 0$, so that the policy improvement will choose initially the policy that maximizes expected immediate reward. By examining the q_i^k, we see that this policy consists of choosing the first alternative in each state. In other words, the policy vector **d** whose ith element is the decision in the ith state is

$$\mathbf{d} = \begin{bmatrix} 1 \\ 1 \\ 1 \end{bmatrix}$$

or the policy is always cruise.

The transition probabilities and expected immediate rewards corresponding to this policy are

$$\mathbf{P} = \begin{bmatrix} \frac{1}{2} & \frac{1}{4} & \frac{1}{4} \\ \frac{1}{2} & 0 & \frac{1}{2} \\ \frac{1}{4} & \frac{1}{4} & \frac{1}{2} \end{bmatrix} \qquad \mathbf{q} = \begin{bmatrix} 8 \\ 16 \\ 7 \end{bmatrix}$$

Now the value-determination operation is entered, and we solve the equations

$$g + v_i = q_i + \sum_{j=1}^{N} p_{ij} v_j \qquad i = 1, 2, \cdots, N$$

In this case we have

$$g + v_1 = 8 + \tfrac{1}{2}v_1 + \tfrac{1}{4}v_2 + \tfrac{1}{4}v_3$$
$$g + v_2 = 16 + \tfrac{1}{2}v_1 + 0v_2 + \tfrac{1}{2}v_3$$
$$g + v_3 = 7 + \tfrac{1}{4}v_1 + \tfrac{1}{4}v_2 + \tfrac{1}{2}v_3$$

Setting $v_3 = 0$ arbitrarily and solving these equations, we obtain

$$v_1 = 1.33 \qquad v_2 = 7.47 \qquad v_3 = 0 \qquad g = 9.2$$

Under a policy of always cruising, the driver will make 9.2 units per trip on the average.

Returning to the policy-improvement routine, we calculate the quantities

$$q_i^k + \sum_{j=1}^{N} p_{ij}^k v_j$$

for all i and k, as shown in Table 5.2.

Table 5.2. FIRST POLICY IMPROVEMENT FOR TAXICAB PROBLEM

State i	Alternative k	Test Quantity $q_i^k + \sum_{j=1}^{N} p_{ij}^k v_j$
1	1	10.53 ←
	2	8.43
	3	5.52
2	1	16.67
	2	21.62 ←
3	1	9.20
	2	9.77 ←
	3	5.97

We see that for $i = 1$ the quantity in the right-hand column is maximized when $k = 1$. For $i = 2$ or 3, it is maximized when $k = 2$. In other words, our new policy is

$$\mathbf{d} = \begin{bmatrix} 1 \\ 2 \\ 2 \end{bmatrix}$$

This means that if the driver is in town A he should cruise; if he is in town B or C, he should drive to the nearest stand.

We have now

$$\mathbf{P} = \begin{bmatrix} \tfrac{1}{2} & \tfrac{1}{4} & \tfrac{1}{4} \\ \tfrac{1}{16} & \tfrac{7}{8} & \tfrac{1}{16} \\ \tfrac{1}{8} & \tfrac{3}{4} & \tfrac{1}{8} \end{bmatrix} \qquad \mathbf{q} = \begin{bmatrix} 8 \\ 15 \\ 4 \end{bmatrix}$$

TAXICAB OPERATION

Returning to the value-determination operation, we solve the equations

$$g + v_1 = 8 + \tfrac{1}{2}v_1 + \tfrac{1}{4}v_2 + \tfrac{1}{4}v_3$$
$$g + v_2 = 15 + \tfrac{1}{16}v_1 + \tfrac{7}{8}v_2 + \tfrac{1}{16}v_3$$
$$g + v_3 = 4 + \tfrac{1}{8}v_1 + \tfrac{3}{4}v_2 + \tfrac{1}{8}v_3$$

Again with $v_3 = 0$, we obtain

$$v_1 = -3.88 \qquad v_2 = 12.85 \qquad v_3 = 0 \qquad g = 13.15$$

Note that g has increased from 9.2 to 13.15 as desired, so that the cab earns 13.15 units per trip on the average. A second policy-improvement routine is shown in Table 5.3.

Table 5.3. SECOND POLICY IMPROVEMENT FOR TAXICAB PROBLEM

State i	Alternative k	Test Quantity $q_i^k + \sum_{j=1}^{N} p_{ij}^k v_j$
1	1	9.27
	2	12.14 ←
	3	4.89
2	1	14.06
	2	26.00 ←
3	1	9.24
	2	13.10 ←
	3	2.39

The new policy is thus

$$\mathbf{d} = \begin{bmatrix} 2 \\ 2 \\ 2 \end{bmatrix}$$

The driver should proceed to the nearest stand, regardless of the town in which he finds himself.

With this policy

$$\mathbf{P} = \begin{bmatrix} \tfrac{1}{16} & \tfrac{3}{4} & \tfrac{3}{16} \\ \tfrac{1}{16} & \tfrac{7}{8} & \tfrac{1}{16} \\ \tfrac{1}{8} & \tfrac{3}{4} & \tfrac{1}{8} \end{bmatrix} \qquad \mathbf{q} = \begin{bmatrix} 2.75 \\ 15 \\ 4 \end{bmatrix}$$

Entering the value-determination operation, we have

$$g + v_1 = 2.75 + \tfrac{1}{16}v_1 + \tfrac{3}{4}v_2 + \tfrac{3}{16}v_3$$
$$g + v_2 = 15 + \tfrac{1}{16}v_1 + \tfrac{7}{8}v_2 + \tfrac{1}{16}v_3$$
$$g + v_3 = 4 + \tfrac{1}{8}v_1 + \tfrac{3}{4}v_2 + \tfrac{1}{8}v_3$$

With $v_3 = 0$, the solution to these equations is

$$v_1 = -1.18 \qquad v_2 = 12.66 \qquad v_3 = 0 \qquad g = 13.34$$

Note that there has been a small but definite increase in g from 13.15 to 13.34; however, we as yet have no evidence that the optimal policy has been found. The next policy improvement is shown in Table 5.4.

Table 5.4. Third Policy Improvement for Taxicab Problem

State i	Alternative k	Test Quantity $q_i^k + \sum_{j=1}^{N} p_{ij}^k v_j$
1	1	10.58
	2	12.17 ←
	3	5.54
2	1	15.41
	2	24.42 ←
3	1	9.87
	2	13.34 ←
	3	4.41

The new policy is

$$\mathbf{d} = \begin{bmatrix} 2 \\ 2 \\ 2 \end{bmatrix}$$

but this is equal to the previous policy, so that the process has converged, and g has attained its maximum, namely, 13.34. The cab driver should drive to the nearest stand in any city. Following this policy will yield a return of 13.34 units per trip on the average, almost half as much again as the policy of always cruising found by maximizing expected immediate reward. The calculations are summarized in Table 5.5.

Table 5.5. Summary of Taxicab Problem Solution

v_1	0	1.33	−3.88	−1.18
v_2	0	7.47	12.85	12.66
v_3	0	0	0	0
g	—	9.20	13.15	13.34
	P ↘ ↗ V	P ↘ ↗ V	P ↘ ↗ V	P ↘
d_1	1	1	2	2
d_2	1	2	2	2 STOP
d_3	1	2	2	2

P indicates that this step takes place in the policy-improvement routine. V indicates that this step takes place in the value-determination operation.

Notice that the optimal policy of always driving to a stand is the *worst* policy in terms of immediate reward. This is roughly equivalent to saying that if a cab driver is to conduct his affairs in the best way he must consider not only the fare from a trip but also the destination of the trip with respect to the expectation of further trips. Any experienced cab driver will verify the wisdom of such reasoning. It often happens in the sequential decision process that the birds in the bush are worth more than the one in the hand.

The policy-improvement routine of Table 5.3 provides us with an opportunity to check Eq. 4.12. The policy changed as a result of this routine from a policy A for which

$$\mathbf{d} = \begin{bmatrix} 1 \\ 2 \\ 2 \end{bmatrix}$$

to a policy B described by

$$\mathbf{d} = \begin{bmatrix} 2 \\ 2 \\ 2 \end{bmatrix}$$

The quantities γ_i defined by Eq. 4.6 may be obtained from Table 5.3. They are the differences between the test quantities for each policy. We find $\gamma_1 = 12.14 - 9.27 = 2.87$, whereas $\gamma_2 = \gamma_3 = 0$ because the decisions in states 2 and 3 are the same for both policies A and B.

Application of Eqs. 1.5 and 1.6 to the transition-probability matrix for policy B yields the limiting state probabilities:

$$\pi_1 = 0.0672 \qquad \pi_2 = 0.8571 \qquad \pi_3 = 0.0757$$

From Eq. 4.12 we then have that

$$g^\Delta = (0.0672)(2.87) = 0.19$$

The change of policy from A to B should thus have produced an increase in gain of 0.19 unit. Since $g^A = 13.15$ and $g^B = 13.34$, our prediction is correct.

A Baseball Problem

It is interesting to explore computational methods of solving the discrete sequential decision problem. The policy-improvement routine is a simple computational problem compared to the value-determination operation. In order to determine the gain and the values, it is necessary to solve a set of simultaneous equations that may be quite large.

A computer program for solving the problem that we have been discussing has been developed as an instrument of research. This program performs the value-determination operation by solving a set of simultaneous equations using the Gauss-Jordan reduction. Problems possessing up to 50 states and with up to 50 alternatives in each state may be solved.

Table 5.6. BASEBALL PROBLEM DATA

1. *Manager tells player at bat to try for a hit.*

Outcome	Probability of Outcome	Batter Goes to	Player on First Goes to	Player on Second Goes to	Player on Third Goes to
Single	0.15	1	2	3	H
Double	0.07	2	3	H	H
Triple	0.05	3	H	H	H
Home run	0.03	H	H	H	H
Base on balls	0.10	1	2	3 (if forced)	H (if forced)
Strike out	0.30	Out	1	2	3
Fly out	0.10	Out	1	2	H (if less than 2 outs)
Ground out	0.10	Out	2	3	H (if less than 2 outs)
Double play	0.10	Out	\multicolumn{4}{The player nearest first is out.}

The interpretation of these outcomes is not described in detail. For instance, if there are no men on base, then hitting into a double play is counted simply as making an out.

2. *Manager tells player at bat to bunt.*

Outcome	Probability	Effect
Single	0.05	Runners advance one base.
Sacrifice	0.60	Batter out; runners advance one base.
Fielder's choice	0.20	Batter safe; runner nearest to making run is out, other runners stay put unless forced.
Strike or foul out	0.10	Batter out; runners do not advance.
Double play	0.05	Batter and player nearest first are out.

3. *Manager tells player on first to steal second.*

4. *Manager tells player on second to steal third.*

In either case, the attempt is successful with probability 0.4, the player's position is unchanged with probability 0.2, and the player is out with probability 0.4.

5. *Manager tells player on third to steal home.*

The outcomes are the same as those above, but the corresponding probabilities are 0.2, 0.1, and 0.7.

Baseball fans please note: No claim is made for the validity of either assumptions or data.

A BASEBALL PROBLEM

When this program was used to solve the taxicab problem, it of course yielded the same solutions we obtained earlier, but with more significant figures. The power of the technique can be appreciated only in a more complex problem possessing several states. As an illustration of such a problem, let us analyze the game of baseball using suitable simplifying assumptions to make the problem manageable.

Consider the half of an inning of a baseball game when one team is at bat. This team is unusual because all its players are identical in athletic ability and their play is unaffected by the tensions of the game. The manager makes all decisions regarding the strategy of the team, and his alternatives are limited in number. He may tell the batter to hit or bunt, tell a man on first to steal second, a man on second to steal third, or a man on third to steal home. For each situation during the inning and for each alternative, there will be a probability of reaching each other situation that could exist and an associated reward expressed in runs. Let us specify the probabilities of transition under each alternative as shown in Table 5.6.

The state of the system depends upon the number of outs and upon the situation on the bases. We may designate the state of the system by a four-digit number $d_1d_2d_3d_4$, where d_1 is the number of outs—0, 1, 2, or 3—and the digits $d_2d_3d_4$ are 1 or 0 corresponding to whether there is or is not a player on bases 3, 2, and 1, respectively. Thus the state designation 2110 would identify the situation "2 outs; players on second and third," where 1111 would mean "1 out; bases loaded." The states are also given a decimal number equal to $1 + 8d_1 +$ (decimal number corresponding to binary number $d_1d_3d_4$). The state 0000 would be state 1, and the state 3000 would be state 25; 2110 corresponds to 23, 1111 to 16. There are eight base situations possible for each of the three out situations 0, 1, 2. There is also the three-out case 3---, where the situation on base is irrelevant and we may arbitrarily call 3---, the state 3000. Therefore, we have a 25-state problem.

The number of alternatives in each state is not the same. State 1000 or 9 has no men on base, so that none of the stealing alternatives are applicable, and only the hit or bunt options are present. State 0101 or 6 has four alternatives: hit, bunt, steal second, or steal home. State 3000 or 25 has only 1 alternative, and that alternative causes it to return to itself with probability 1 and reward 0. State 25 is a trapping or recurrent state; it is the only state that the system may occupy as the number of transitions becomes infinite.

To fix ideas still more clearly, let us list explicitly in Table 5.7 the transition probabilities $p_{ij}{}^k$ and rewards $r_{ij}{}^k$ for a typical state, say 0011 or 4. In state $4(i = 4)$, three alternatives apply: hit, bunt, steal third. Only nonzero $p_{ij}{}^k$ are listed. The highest expected immediate reward in this state would be obtained by following alternative 1, Hit.

Table 5.7. PROBABILITIES AND REWARDS FOR STATE 4 OF BASEBALL PROBLEM (0011)

First alternative: Hit, $k = 1$.

Next State	j	$p_{4j}{}^1$	$r_{4j}{}^1$	
0000	1	0.03	3	
0100	5	0.05	2	
0110	7	0.07	1	
0111	8	0.25	0	$q_4{}^1 = 0.26$
1011	12	0.40	0	
1110	15	0.10	0	
2010	19	0.10	0	

Second alternative: Bunt, $k = 2$.

Next State	j	$p_{4j}{}^2$	$r_{4j}{}^2$	
0111	8	0.05	0	
1011	12	0.30	0	$q_4{}^2 = 0$
1110	15	0.60	0	
2010	19	0.05	0	

Third alternative: Steal third, $k = 3$.

Next State	j	$p_{4j}{}^3$	$r_{4j}{}^3$	
0011	4	0.20	0	
0101	6	0.40	0	$q_4{}^3 = 0$
1001	10	0.40	0	

Table 5.8, entitled "Summary of Baseball Problem Input," shows for each state i the state description, the alternatives open to the manager in that state, and $q_i{}^k$, the expected immediate reward (in runs) from following alternative k in state i. The final column shows the policy that would be obtained by maximizing expected immediate reward in each state. This policy is to bunt in states 5, 6, 13, and 14, and to hit in all others. States 5, 6, 13, and 14 may be described as those states with a player on third, none on second, and with less than two outs.

The foregoing data were used as an input to the computer program described earlier. Since the program chooses an initial policy by maximizing expected immediate reward, the initial policy was the one just mentioned. The machine had to solve the equations only twice to reach a solution. Its results are summarized in Table 5.9.

The optimal policy is to hit in every state. The v_i may be interpreted as the expected number of runs that will be made if the inning is now in state i and it is played until three outs are incurred. Since a team

Table 5.8. Summary of Baseball Problem Input

i	State Description Outs	Bases 3	2	1	Alternative 1 $k=1$ q_i^1	Alternative 2 $k=2$ q_i^2	Alternative 3 $k=3$ q_i^3	Alternative 4 $k=4$ q_i^4	Number of Alternatives in State i	Initial Policy d_i if v_i Set = 0
1	0	0	0	0	0.03 Hit	—	—	—	1	1
2	0	0	0	1	0.11 Hit	0 Bunt	0 Steal 2	—	3	1
3	0	0	1	0	0.18 Hit	0 Bunt	0 Steal 3	—	3	1
4	0	0	1	1	0.26 Hit	0 Bunt	0 Steal 3	—	3	1
5	0	1	0	0	0.53 Hit	0.65 Bunt	0.20 Steal H	—	3	2
6	0	1	0	1	0.61 Hit	0.65 Bunt	0 Steal 2	0.20 Steal H	4	2
7	0	1	1	0	0.68 Hit	0.65 Bunt	0.20 Steal H	—	3	1
8	0	1	1	1	0.86 Hit	0.65 Bunt	0.20 Steal H	—	3	1
9	1	0	0	0	0.03 Hit	—	—	—	1	1
10	1	0	0	1	0.11 Hit	0 Bunt	0 Steal 2	—	3	1
11	1	0	1	0	0.18 Hit	0 Bunt	0 Steal 3	—	3	1
12	1	0	1	1	0.26 Hit	0 Bunt	0 Steal 3	—	3	1
13	1	1	0	0	0.53 Hit	0.65 Bunt	0.20 Steal H	—	3	2
14	1	1	0	1	0.61 Hit	0.65 Bunt	0 Steal 2	0.20 Steal H	4	2
15	1	1	1	0	0.68 Hit	0.65 Bunt	0.20 Steal H	—	3	1
16	1	1	1	1	0.86 Hit	0.65 Bunt	0.20 Steal H	—	3	1
17	2	0	0	0	0.03 Hit	—	—	—	1	1
18	2	0	0	1	0.11 Hit	0 Bunt	0 Steal 2	—	3	1
19	2	0	1	0	0.18 Hit	0 Bunt	0 Steal 3	—	3	1
20	2	0	1	1	0.26 Hit	0 Bunt	0 Steal 3	—	3	1
21	2	1	0	0	0.33 Hit	0.05 Bunt	0.20 Steal H	—	3	1
22	2	1	0	1	0.41 Hit	0.05 Bunt	0 Steal 2	0.20 Steal H	4	1
23	2	1	1	0	0.48 Hit	0.05 Bunt	0.20 Steal H	—	3	1
24	2	1	1	1	0.66 Hit	0.05 Bunt	0.20 Steal H	—	3	1
25	3	—	—	—	0 Trapped	—	—	—	1	1

starts each inning in state 1, or "no outs, no men on," then v_1 may be interpreted as the expected number of runs per inning under the given policy. The initial policy yields 0.75 for v_1, whereas the optimal policy yields 0.81. In other words, the team will earn about 0.06 more runs per inning on the average if it uses the optimal policy rather than the policy that maximizes expected immediate reward.

Note that under both policies the gain was zero as expected, since after an infinite number of moves the system will be in state 25 and will always make reward 0. Note also that, in spite of the fact that the gain could not be increased, the policy-improvement routine yielded values for the optimal policy that are all greater than or equal to those for the initial policy. The appendix shows that the policy-improvement routine will maximize values if it is impossible to increase gain.

The values v_i can be used in comparing the usefulness of states. For example, under either policy the manager would rather be in a position with two men out and bases loaded than be starting a new inning (compare v_{24} with v_1). However, he would rather start a new inning than have two men out and men on second and third (compare v_{23} with v_1). Many other interesting comparisons can be made. Under the optimal policy, having no men out and a player on first is just about as valuable a position as having one man out and players on first and second (compare v_2 with v_{12}). It is interesting to see how the preceding comparisons compare with our intuitive notions of the relative values of baseball positions.

Table 5.9. Summary of Baseball Problem Solution

	Iteration 1 $g = 0$				Iteration 2 $g = 0$		
State	Description	Decision	Value v_i	State	Description	Decision	Value v_i
1	0000	Hit	0.75	1	0000	Hit	0.81
2	0001	Hit	1.08	2	0001	Hit	1.25
3	0010	Hit	1.18	3	0010	Hit	1.35
4	0011	Hit	1.82	4	0011	Hit	1.89
5	0100	Bunt	1.18	5	0100	Hit	1.56
6	0101	Bunt	1.56	6	0101	Hit	2.07
7	0110	Hit	2.00	7	0110	Hit	2.17
8	0111	Hit	2.67	8	0111	Hit	2.74
9	1000	Hit	0.43	9	1000	Hit	0.46
10	1001	Hit	0.75	10	1001	Hit	0.77
11	1010	Hit	0.79	11	1010	Hit	0.86
12	1011	Hit	1.21	12	1011	Hit	1.23
13	1100	Bunt	0.88	13	1100	Hit	1.11
14	1101	Bunt	1.10	14	1101	Hit	1.44
15	1110	Hit	1.46	15	1110	Hit	1.53
16	1111	Hit	1.93	16	1111	Hit	1.95
17	2000	Hit	0.17	17	2000	Hit	0.17
18	2001	Hit	0.34	18	2001	Hit	0.34
19	2010	Hit	0.40	19	2010	Hit	0.40
20	2011	Hit	0.59	20	2011	Hit	0.59
21	2100	Hit	0.51	21	2100	Hit	0.51
22	2101	Hit	0.68	22	2101	Hit	0.68
23	2110	Hit	0.74	23	2110	Hit	0.74
24	2111	Hit	0.99	24	2111	Hit	0.99
25	3000	Hit	0	25	3000	Hit	0

The Replacement Problem

The examples of the policy-iteration method presented up to this point have been somewhat far removed from the realm of practical problems. It would be extremely interesting to see the method applied to a problem that is of major importance to industry. As an example of such a practical application, the replacement problem was chosen. This is the problem of when to replace a piece of capital equipment that deteriorates with time. The question to be answered is this: If we now own a machine of a certain age, should we keep it or should we trade it in; further, if we trade it in, how old a machine should we buy?

In order to fix ideas, let us consider the problem of automobile

THE REPLACEMENT PROBLEM

replacement over a time interval of ten years. We agree to review our current situation every three months and to make a decision on keeping our present car or trading it in at that time. The state of the system, i, is described by the age of the car in three-month periods; i may run from 1 to 40. In order to keep the number of states finite, a car of age 40 remains a car of age 40 forever (it is considered to be essentially worn out). The alternatives available in each state are these: The first alternative, $k = 1$, is to keep the present car for another quarter. The other alternatives, $k > 1$, are to buy a car of age $k - 2$, where $k - 2$ may be as large as 39. We have then 40 states with 41 alternatives in each state, with the result that there are 41^{40} possible policies.

The data supplied are the following:

C_i, the cost of buying a car of age i
T_i, the trade-in value of a car of age i
E_i, the expected cost of operating a car of age i until it reaches age $i + 1$
p_i, the probability that a car of age i will survive to be age $i + 1$ without incurring a prohibitively expensive repair

The probability defined here is necessary to limit the number of states. A car of any age that has a hopeless breakdown is immediately sent to state 40. Naturally, $p_{40} = 0$.

The basic equations governing the system when it is in state i are the following: If $k = 1$ (keep present car),

$$g + v_i = -E_i + p_i v_{i+1} + (1 - p_i)v_{40}$$

If $k > 1$ (trade for car of age $k - 2$),

$$g + v_i = T_i - C_{k-2} - E_{k-2} + p_{k-2}v_{k-1} + (1 - p_{k-2})v_{40}$$

It is simple to phrase these equations in terms of our earlier notation. For instance,

$$q_i^k = -E_i \quad \text{for } k = 1 \qquad q_i^k = T_i - C_{k-2} - E_{k-2} \quad \text{for } k > 1$$

$$p_{ij}^k = \begin{cases} p_i & j = i + 1 \\ 1 - p_i & j = 40 \\ 0 & \text{other } j \end{cases} \quad \text{for } k = 1$$

$$p_{ij}^k = \begin{cases} p_{k-2} & j = k - 1 \\ 1 - p_{k-2} & j = 40 \\ 0 & \text{other } j \end{cases} \quad \text{for } k > 1$$

EXAMPLES OF THE METHOD

The actual data used in the problem are listed in Table 5.10 and graphed in Figure 5.1. The discontinuities in the cost and trade-in functions were introduced in order to characterize typical model-year effects.

Table 5.10. AUTOMOBILE REPLACEMENT DATA

Age in Periods i	Cost C_i	Trade-in Value T_i	Operating Expense E_i	Survival Probability p_i	Age in Periods i	Cost C_i	Trade-in Value T_i	Operating Expense E_i	Survival Probability p_i
0	$2000	$1600	$50	1.000					
1	1840	1460	53	0.999	21	$345	$240	$115	0.925
2	1680	1340	56	0.998	22	330	225	118	0.919
3	1560	1230	59	0.997	23	315	210	121	0.910
4	1300	1050	62	0.996	24	300	200	125	0.900
5	1220	980	65	0.994	25	290	190	129	0.890
6	1150	910	68	0.991	26	280	180	133	0.880
7	1080	840	71	0.988	27	265	170	137	0.865
8	900	710	75	0.985	28	250	160	141	0.850
9	840	650	78	0.983	29	240	150	145	0.820
10	780	600	81	0.980	30	230	145	150	0.790
11	730	550	84	0.975	31	220	140	155	0.760
12	600	480	87	0.970	32	210	135	160	0.730
13	560	430	90	0.965	33	200	130	167	0.660
14	520	390	93	0.960	34	190	120	175	0.590
15	480	360	96	0.955	35	180	115	182	0.510
16	440	330	100	0.950	36	170	110	190	0.430
17	420	310	103	0.945	37	160	105	205	0.300
18	400	290	106	0.940	38	150	95	220	0.200
19	380	270	109	0.935	39	140	87	235	0.100
20	360	255	112	0.930	40	130	80	250	0

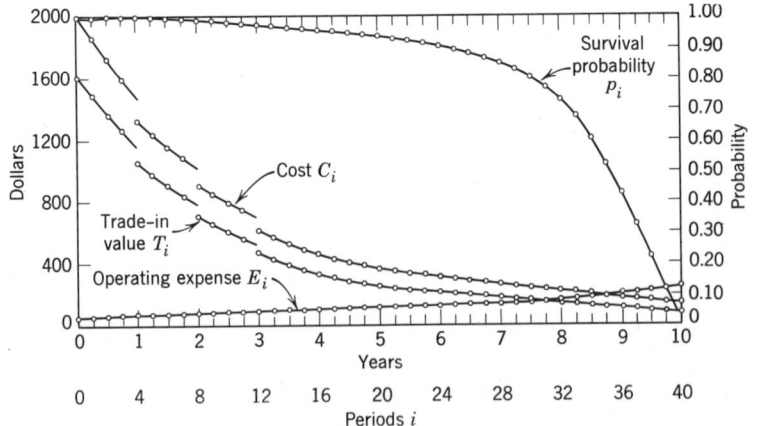

Fig. 5.1. Automobile replacement data.

THE REPLACEMENT PROBLEM

The automobile replacement problem was solved by the policy-iteration method in seven iterations. The sequence of policies, gains, and values is shown in Table 5.11. The optimal policy given by iteration 7 is this: If you have a car that is more than $\frac{1}{2}$ year old but less than $6\frac{1}{2}$ years old, keep it. If you have a car of any other age, trade it in on a 3-year-old car. This seems to correspond quite well with our intuitive notions concerning the economics of automobile ownership. Note that if we at present have a car that is 3 or 6 months old we should trade it for a 3-year-old car, but that if our car's age is between 6 months and $6\frac{1}{2}$ years, we should keep it. These rules enable us to enter the 3 to $6\frac{1}{2}$ cycle; once the cycle is entered, the car we own will always be between 3 and $6\frac{1}{4}$ years old.* It is satisfying to note that the program at any iteration requires that, if we are going to trade, we must trade for a car whose age is independent of our present car's age. This is just the result that the logic of the situation would dictate.

If we follow our optimal policy, we shall keep a car until it is $6\frac{1}{2}$ years old and then buy a 3-year-old car. Suppose, however, that when our car is 4 years old, a friend offers to swap his 1-year-old car for ours for an amount X. Should we take up his offer? In order to answer this question, we must look at the values.

In each of the iterations, the value of state 40 was set equal to zero for computational purposes. Table 5.11 also shows the values under the best policy when the value of state 40 is set equal to $80, the trade-in value of a car of that age. When this is done, each v_i represents the value of a car of age i to a person who is following the optimal policy. In order to answer the question just posed, we must compare the value of a 1-year-old car, $v_4 = \$1152$, with the value of a 4-year-old car, $v_{16} = \$422$. If his asking price X is less than $v_4 - v_{16} = \$730$, we should make the trade; otherwise, we should not. It is, of course, not necessary to change v_{40} from zero in order to answer this problem; however, making $v_{40} = \$80$ does give the values an absolute physical interpretation as well as a relative one.

If the optimal policy is followed, the yearly cost of transportation is about $604 (4 × $150.95). If the policy of maximizing immediate reward shown in iteration 1 were followed, the yearly cost would be $1000. Thus, following a policy that maximizes future reward

---

* Of course, chaos for the automobile industry would result if everyone followed this policy. Where would the 3-year-old cars come from? Economic forces would increase the price of such cars to a point where the 3 to $6\frac{1}{2}$ policy is no longer optimal. The preceding analysis must assume that there are enough people in the market buying cars for psychological reasons that so-called "rational" buyers are a negligible influence.

Table 5.11. AUTOMOBILE REPLACEMENT RESULTS

State	Iteration 1 Gain: –$250.00 Decision	Value	Iteration 2 Gain: –$193.89 Decision	Value	Iteration 3 Gain: –$162.44 Decision	Value	Iteration 4 Gain: –$157.07 Decision	Value	Iteration 5 Gain: –$151.05 Decision	Value	Iteration 6 Gain: –$150.99 Decision	Value	Iteration 7 Gain: –$150.95 Decision	Value	Adjusted Value
1	36	$1374	20	$1380	19	$1380	12	$1380	12	$1380	12	$1380	12	$1380	$1460
2	36	1254	20	1260	19	1260	12	1260	12	1260	12	1260	12	1260	1340
3	36	1144	20	1150	19	1150	12	1150	12	1150	12	1150	K	1161	1241
4	36	964	20	970	K	1037	12	970	K	1003	K	1072	K	1072	1152
5	36	894	20	900	K	940	12	900	K	917	K	987	K	987	1067
6	36	824	20	830	K	848	12	830	K	836	K	907	K	906	986
7	36	754	20	760	19	760	12	760	12	760	K	831	K	831	911
8	36	624	20	630	K	696	12	630	K	761	K	760	K	760	840
9	36	564	20	570	K	617	12	570	K	695	K	695	K	695	775
10	36	514	20	520	K	542	12	520	K	633	K	633	K	632	712
11	36	464	20	470	K	470	12	470	K	574	K	574	K	574	654
12	36	394	20	400	19	400	K	520	K	520	K	520	K	520	600
13	36	344	20	350	K	575	K	464	K	470	K	470	K	470	550
14	36	304	20	310	K	521	K	411	K	424	K	424	K	424	504
15	36	274	20	280	K	470	K	362	K	381	K	381	K	381	461
16	36	244	20	250	K	423	K	315	K	341	K	342	K	342	422
17	36	224	20	230	K	380	K	271	K	306	K	306	K	306	386
18	36	204	20	210	K	338	K	230	K	273	K	273	K	273	353
19	36	184	20	190	K	300	K	190	K	242	K	243	K	243	323
20	36	169	K	280	K	264	12	175	K	214	K	214	K	215	295
21	K	876	K	213	K	229	12	160	K	188	K	189	K	189	269
22	K	801	20	145	K	197	12	145	K	164	K	165	K	166	246
23	K	728	20	130	K	166	12	130	K	143	K	144	K	144	224
24	K	658	20	120	K	136	12	120	K	124	K	125	K	126	206
25	K	592	20	110	19	110	12	110	K	109	K	110	12	111	191
26	K	530	20	100	19	100	12	100	K	97	12	100	12	100	180
27	K	469	20	90	19	90	12	90	12	90	12	90	12	90	170
28	K	412	20	80	19	80	12	80	12	80	12	80	12	80	160
29	K	356	20	70	19	70	12	70	12	70	12	70	12	70	150
30	K	306	20	65	19	65	12	65	12	65	12	65	12	65	145
31	K	261	20	60	19	60	12	60	12	60	12	60	12	60	140
32	K	218	20	55	19	55	12	55	12	55	12	55	12	55	135
33	K	176	20	50	19	50	12	50	12	50	12	50	12	50	130
34	K	140	20	40	19	40	12	40	12	40	12	40	12	40	120
35	K	111	20	35	19	35	12	35	12	35	12	35	12	35	115
36	K	84	20	30	19	30	12	30	12	30	12	30	12	30	110
37	K	55	20	25	19	25	12	25	12	25	12	25	12	25	105
38	K	33	20	15	19	15	12	15	12	15	12	15	12	15	95
39	K	15	20	7	19	7	12	7	12	7	12	7	12	7	87
40	K	0	20	0	19	0	12	0	12	0	12	0	12	0	80

A number in the decision column means trade for a car of that age in periods; a K means keep the present car. Values and gains are expressed in dollars. The adjusted value is computed by adding $80, the value of a scrap car, to each of the Iteration 7 values.

rather than immediate reward has resulted in a saving of almost $400 per year. The decrease of period cost with iteration is shown in Fig. 5.2. The gain approaches the optimal value roughly exponentially. Notice that the gains for the last three iterations are so close that for all practical purposes the corresponding policies may be considered

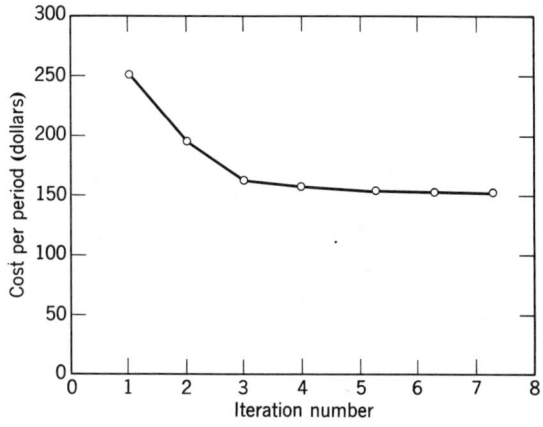

Fig. 5.2. Quarterly cost of automobile operation as a function of iteration.

to be equivalent. The fact that a 3-year-old car is the best buy is discovered as early as iteration 4. The model-year discontinuity occurring at 3 years is no doubt responsible for this particular selection.

The replacement problem described in this section is typical of a large class of industrial replacement problems. Placing these problems in the framework of the policy-iteration method requires only a thorough understanding of their peculiarities and some foresight in selecting a suitable formulation.

6

The Policy-Iteration Method for Multiple-Chain Processes

The developments of Chapter 4 assumed that all the possible policies for the system were completely ergodic. Complete ergodicity meant that each policy defined a Markov process with only one recurrent chain, and thus with a unique gain. Our problem was simply to find the policy that had highest gain; the method of Chapter 4 accomplished this purpose. This iteration technique is satisfactory for most problems because we can usually define a problem in such a way as to meet the requirement that it have only completely ergodic policies. This was the case for the examples of Chapter 5.

However, it is not difficult to think of processes that have multiple chains. In Chapter 1 we discussed a three-state process with transition-probability matrix

$$\mathbf{P} = \begin{bmatrix} 1 & 0 & 0 \\ 0 & 1 & 0 \\ \frac{1}{3} & \frac{1}{3} & \frac{1}{3} \end{bmatrix}$$

that had two recurrent chains. Suppose that the process had an expected immediate reward vector $\mathbf{q} = \begin{bmatrix} 1 \\ 2 \\ 3 \end{bmatrix}$ expressed in dollars. The matrix of limiting-state probability vectors was found in Chapter 1 to be

$$\mathbf{S} = \begin{bmatrix} 1 & 0 & 0 \\ 0 & 1 & 0 \\ \frac{1}{2} & \frac{1}{2} & 0 \end{bmatrix}$$

The gain vector $\mathbf{g} = \mathbf{Sq} = \begin{bmatrix} 1 \\ 2 \\ 1.5 \end{bmatrix}$, and we interpret $\mathbf{g}$ as follows: If the process were started in state 1, it would earn $1.00 per transition. A start in state 2 would earn $2.00 per transition. Finally, since the system is equally likely to enter state 1 or state 2 after many transitions if it is started in state 3, such a starting position is expected to earn $1.50 per transition on the average. The averaging involved is performed over several independent trials starting in state 3, because in any given trial either $1.00 or $2.00 per transition will be ultimately earned.

The gain of the system thus depends upon the state in which it is started. A start in state i produces a gain g_i, so that we may think of the gain as being a function of the state as well as of the process. Our new task is to find the policy for the system that will maximize the gain of *all* states of the system. We are fortunate that the policy-iteration method of Chapter 4 can be extended to the case of multiple-gain processes. We shall now proceed to this extension.

The Value-Determination Operation

Equations 2.15 show the asymptotic form that the total expected reward of the system assumes when the system is started in state i and allowed to make a large number of transitions:

$$v_i(n) = n g_i + v_i \qquad i = 1, 2, \cdots, N \tag{2.15}$$

Each state has its own g_i, but, as discussed in Chapter 2, all states that are members of the same recurrent chain have the same gain. If we agree to study the unending process, Eqs. 2.15 may be used with the basic recurrence relation for total expected earnings,

$$v_i(n+1) = q_i + \sum_{j=1}^{N} p_{ij} v_j(n) \qquad i = 1, 2, \cdots, N \tag{6.1}$$

to yield

$$(n+1)g_i + v_i = q_i + \sum_{j=1}^{N} p_{ij}(n g_j + v_j)$$

or

$$n g_i + g_i + v_i = q_i + n \sum_{j=1}^{N} p_{ij} g_j + \sum_{j=1}^{N} p_{ij} v_j \tag{6.2}$$

If Eq. 6.2 is to be satisfied for any large n, it follows that

$$g_i = \sum_{j=1}^{N} p_{ij} g_j \qquad i = 1, 2, \cdots, N \tag{6.3}$$

and

$$g_i + v_i = q_i + \sum_{j=1}^{N} p_{ij} v_j \qquad i = 1, 2, \cdots, N \qquad (6.4)$$

We now have the two sets of N linear simultaneous equations (Eqs. 6.3 and 6.4) that we may use to solve for the Ng_i and Nv_i. However, Eqs. 6.3 may not be solved uniquely for the g_i. The matrix $[\mathbf{I} - \mathbf{P}]$ has a singular determinant, so that the solution for the g_i obtained from Eqs. 6.3 will contain arbitrary constants. The number of arbitrary constants is equal to the number of recurrent chains in the process. Equations 6.3 essentially relate the gains of each state to the gains of each recurrent chain. For example, in an L-chain process there will be L independent gains. The gains of the states that are transient will be related by Eqs. 6.3 to the L independent gains and so will be determined when the independent gains are determined.

The N equations (Eqs. 6.4) must now be used to determine the L independent gains and also the Nv_i. We thus have L too many unknowns. However, suppose that we extend our former procedure by setting equal to zero the v_i for one state in each recurrent chain, so that a total of Lv_i will be equated to zero. We shall generally choose the highest numbered state in each chain to be the one whose v_i is set equal to zero. We find that Eqs. 6.4 may now be solved for the L independent gains and for the remaining $(N - L)v_i$.

The v_i determined by the solution of Eqs. 6.4 may still be called relative values if we remember that they are relative within a chain. The difficulty of solving Eqs. 6.3 and 6.4 is about the same as that of finding the limiting-state-probability matrix $\mathbf{S}$ for a multiple-chain process. We shall see that the relative values v_i are as useful as the true limiting v_i defined by Eqs. 2.15, as far as the search for the optimal policy is concerned.

To illustrate these remarks, let us find the gain and relative values of the two-chain process discussed at the beginning of this section. Equations 6.3. yield

$$g_1 = g_1 \qquad g_2 = g_2 \qquad g_3 = \tfrac{1}{3}g_1 + \tfrac{1}{3}g_2 + \tfrac{1}{3}g_3$$

Thus there are two independent gains g_1 and g_2. The gain of state 3 is expressed in terms of g_1 and g_2 by $g_3 = \tfrac{1}{2}g_1 + \tfrac{1}{2}g_2$. If we could find g_1 and g_2, we should know the gain of every state. In general, we shall call ^1g the gain of chain 1, ^2g the gain of 2, and so on, and then express the gain of each state in terms of $^1g, ^2g, \cdots$. This notation cannot be used until the states are identified with respect to chain membership. For this problem, $g_1 = {}^1g$, $g_2 = {}^2g$, and $g_3 = \tfrac{1}{2}{}^1g + \tfrac{1}{2}{}^2g$.

Equations 6.4 yield

$$g_1 + v_1 = 1 + v_1 \qquad g_2 + v_2 = 2 + v_2$$
$$g_3 + v_3 = 3 + \tfrac{1}{3}v_1 + \tfrac{1}{3}v_2 + \tfrac{1}{3}v_3$$

If we now express g_3 in terms of g_1 and g_2 and then set equal to zero the relative value of one state in each recurrent chain so that $v_1 = v_2 = 0$, we obtain

$$g_1 = 1 \qquad g_2 = 2 \qquad \tfrac{1}{3}g_1 + \tfrac{1}{3}g_2 + v_3 = 3 + \tfrac{1}{3}v_3$$

The solution of this set of equations is $g_1 = 1$, $g_2 = 2$, $v_3 = 2.25$, so that

$$g_1 = 1 \qquad g_2 = 2 \qquad g_3 = 1.5$$
$$v_1 = 0 \qquad v_2 = 0 \qquad v_3 = 2.25$$

are the gains and relative values for each state of the process. The gains are of course the same as those obtained earlier.

The Policy-Improvement Routine

We shall now show how the gains and the relative values of a policy may be used to find the optimal policy for the system. Following the argument of Chapter 4, if we now have a policy that we have been following up to stage n, we may find a better decision for the ith state at stage $n + 1$ by maximizing

$$q_i^k + \sum_{j=1}^{N} p_{ij}^k v_j(n) \qquad (4.2)$$

with respect to all alternatives in state i. For large n, in Expression 4.2 we may substitute the relation in Eqs. 2.15 to obtain

$$q_i^k + \sum_{j=1}^{N} p_{ij}^k (n g_j + v_j)$$

or

$$n \sum_{j=1}^{N} p_{ij}^k g_j + q_i^k + \sum_{j=1}^{N} p_{ij}^k v_j \qquad (6.5)$$

as the test quantity to be maximized. When n is large, Expression 6.5 is of course maximized by the alternative that maximizes

$$\sum_{j=1}^{N} p_{ij}^k g_j$$

Policy Evaluation

Use p_{ij} and q_i for a given policy to solve the double set of equations

$$g_i = \sum_{j=1}^{N} p_{ij} g_j \qquad i = 1, 2, \cdots, N$$

$$v_i + g_i = q_i + \sum_{j=1}^{N} p_{ij} v_j \qquad i = 1, 2, \cdots, N$$

for all v_i and g_i, by setting the value of one v_i in each recurrent chain to zero.

Policy Improvement

For each state i, determine the alternative k that maximizes

$$\sum_{j=1}^{N} p_{ij}{}^k g_j$$

using the gains of the previous policy, and make it the new decision in the ith state.
If

$$\sum_{j=1}^{N} p_{ij}{}^k g_j$$

is the same for all alternatives, or if several alternatives are equally good according to this test, the decision must be made on the basis of relative values rather than gains. Therefore, if the gain test fails, break the tie by determining the alternative k that maximizes

$$q_i{}^k + \sum_{j=1}^{N} p_{ij}{}^k v_j$$

using the relative values of the previous policy, and by making it the new decision in the ith state.

Regardless of whether the policy-improvement test is based on gains or values, if the old decision in the ith state yields as high a value of the test quantity as any other alternative, leave the old decision unchanged. This rule assures convergence in the case of equivalent policies.

When this procedure has been repeated for all states, a new policy has been determined and new $[p_{ij}]$ and $[q_i]$ matrices have been obtained. If the new policy is the same as the previous one, the iteration process has converged, and the best policy has been found; otherwise, enter the upper box.

Fig. 6.1. General iteration cycle for discrete sequential decision processes.

the gain test quantity, using the gains of the old policy. However, when all alternatives have the same value of

$$\sum_{j=1}^{N} p_{ij}{}^{k} g_j$$

or when a group of alternatives have the same maximum value of the gain test quantity, the tie is broken by choosing the alternative that maximizes the value test quantity,

$$q_i{}^k + \sum_{j=1}^{N} p_{ij}{}^{k} v_j$$

by using the relative values of the old policy. The relative values may be used for the value test because, as we shall see, the test is not affected by a constant added to the v_i of all states in a recurrent chain.

The general iteration cycle is shown in Fig. 6.1. Note that it reduces to our iteration cycle of Fig. 4.2 for completely ergodic processes. An example with more than one chain will now be discussed, followed by the relevant proofs of optimality.

A Multichain Example

Let us find the optimal policy for the three-state system whose transition probabilities and rewards are shown in Table 6.1. The transition probabilities are all 1 or 0, first for ease of calculation and second to show that no difficulties are introduced by such a structure. This system has the possibility of multiple-chain policies.

Table 6.1. A MULTICHAIN EXAMPLE

State i	Alternative k	Probabilities $p_{i1}{}^k$	$p_{i2}{}^k$	$p_{i3}{}^k$	Expected Immediate Reward $q_i{}^k$
1	1	1	0	0	1
	2	0	1	0	2
	3	0	0	1	3
2	1	1	0	0	6
	2	0	1	0	4
	3	0	0	1	5
3	1	1	0	0	8
	2	0	1	0	9
	3	0	0	1	7

Let us begin with the policy that maximizes expected immediate reward. This policy is composed of the third alternative in the first state, the first alternative in the second state, and the second alternative in the third state. For this policy

$$\mathbf{d} = \begin{bmatrix} 3 \\ 1 \\ 2 \end{bmatrix} \qquad \mathbf{P} = \begin{bmatrix} 0 & 0 & 1 \\ 1 & 0 & 0 \\ 0 & 1 & 0 \end{bmatrix} \qquad \mathbf{q} = \begin{bmatrix} 3 \\ 6 \\ 9 \end{bmatrix}$$

We are now ready to enter the policy-evaluation part of the iteration cycle. Equations 6.3 yield

$$g_1 = g_3 \qquad g_2 = g_1 \qquad g_3 = g_2$$

These results show that there is only one recurrent chain and that all three states are members of it. If we call its gain g, then $g_1 = g_2 = g_3 = g$; the relative value v_3 is arbitrarily set equal to zero. If we use these results in writing Eqs. 6.4, the following equations are obtained:

$$g + v_1 = 3 \qquad g + v_2 = 6 + v_1 \qquad g = 9 + v_2$$

Their solution is $g = 6$, $v_1 = v_2 = -3$, so that

$$g_1 = 6 \qquad g_2 = 6 \qquad g_3 = 6$$

and

$$v_1 = -3 \qquad v_2 = -3 \qquad v_3 = 0$$

We are now ready to seek a policy improvement as shown in Table 6.2.

Table 6.2. First Policy Improvement for Multichain Example

State i	Alternative k	Gain Test Quantity $\sum_{j=1}^{N} p_{ij}{}^{k} g_j$	Value Test Quantity $q_i{}^k + \sum_{j=1}^{N} p_{ij}{}^{k} v_j$
1	1	6	$1 + (-3) = -2$
	2	6	$2 + (-3) = -1$
	3	6	$3 + (0) = 3\leftarrow$
2	1	6	$6 + (-3) = 3$
	2	6	$4 + (-3) = 1$
	3	6	$5 + (0) = 5\leftarrow$
3	1	6	$8 + (-3) = 5$
	2	6	$9 + (-3) = 6$
	3	6	$7 + (0) = 7\leftarrow$

Since the gain test produced ties in all cases, the value test was necessary. The new policy is

$$\mathbf{d} = \begin{bmatrix} 3 \\ 3 \\ 3 \end{bmatrix} \qquad \mathbf{P} = \begin{bmatrix} 0 & 0 & 1 \\ 0 & 0 & 1 \\ 0 & 0 & 1 \end{bmatrix} \qquad \mathbf{q} = \begin{bmatrix} 3 \\ 5 \\ 7 \end{bmatrix}$$

This policy must now be evaluated. Equations 6.3 yield

$$g_1 = g_3 \qquad g_2 = g_3 \qquad g_3 = g_3$$

We may let $g_1 = g_2 = g_3 = g$, set $v_3 = 0$, and use Eqs. 6.4 to obtain

$$g + v_1 = 3 \qquad g + v_2 = 5 \qquad g = 7$$

The solution is $g = 7$, $v_1 = -4$, $v_2 = -2$, and so

$$g_1 = 7 \qquad g_2 = 7 \qquad g_3 = 7$$

and

$$v_1 = -4 \qquad v_2 = -2 \qquad v_3 = 0$$

The policy-improvement routine is shown in Table 6.3.

Table 6.3. SECOND POLICY IMPROVEMENT FOR MULTICHAIN EXAMPLE

State i	Alternative k	Gain Test Quantity $\sum_{j=1}^{N} p_{ij}^{k} g_j$	Value Test Quantity $q_i^k + \sum_{j=1}^{N} p_{ij}^{k} v_j$
1	1	7	−3
	2	7	0
	3	7	3 ←
2	1	7	2
	2	7	2
	3	7	5 ←
3	1	7	4
	2	7	7
	3	7	7 ←

Since once more the gain test was indeterminate, it was necessary to rely on the relative-value comparison. In state 3, alternatives 2 and 3 are tied in the value test. However, because alternative 3 was our old decision, it will remain as our new decision. We have thus obtained the same policy twice in succession; it must therefore be the optimal policy. The optimal policy has a gain of 7 in all states. The policy $\mathbf{d} = \begin{bmatrix} 3 \\ 3 \\ 2 \end{bmatrix}$, which was possible because of the equality of the value test in state 3, is also optimal.

Although this system had the capacity for multichain behavior, such behavior did not appear if we chose as our starting point the policy that maximized expected immediate reward. Nevertheless, other choices of starting policy will create this behavior.

Let us assume the following initial policy:

$$\mathbf{d} = \begin{bmatrix} 3 \\ 2 \\ 1 \end{bmatrix} \qquad \mathbf{P} = \begin{bmatrix} 0 & 0 & 1 \\ 0 & 1 & 0 \\ 1 & 0 & 0 \end{bmatrix} \qquad \mathbf{q} = \begin{bmatrix} 3 \\ 4 \\ 8 \end{bmatrix}$$

To evaluate this policy, we first apply Eqs. 6.3 and obtain

$$g_1 = g_3 \qquad g_2 = g_2 \qquad g_3 = g_1$$

There are two recurrent chains. Chain 1 is composed of states 1 and 3, chain 2 of state 2 alone. Therefore, $g_1 = g_3 = {}^1g$, $g_2 = {}^2g$, and we may set $v_2 = v_3 = 0$. Equations 6.4 then yield

$$^1g + v_1 = 3 \qquad {}^2g = 4 \qquad {}^1g = 8 + v_1$$

The solution of these equations is ${}^1g = \frac{11}{2}$, ${}^2g = 4$, $v_1 = -\frac{5}{2}$, and so

$$g_1 = \tfrac{11}{2} \qquad g_2 = 4 \qquad g_3 = \tfrac{11}{2}$$

and

$$v_1 = -\tfrac{5}{2} \qquad v_2 = 0 \qquad v_3 = 0$$

Table 6.4 shows the policy-improvement routine.

Table 6.4. POLICY IMPROVEMENT BY A CHANGE IN CHAIN STRUCTURE

State i	Alternative k	Gain Test Quantity $\sum_{j=1}^{N} p_{ij}{}^k g_j$	Value Test Quantity $q_i{}^k + \sum_{j=1}^{N} p_{ij}{}^k v_j$
1	1	$\tfrac{11}{2}$	$-\tfrac{3}{2}$
	2	4	2
	3	$\tfrac{11}{2}$	3 ←
2	1	$\tfrac{11}{2}$	$\tfrac{7}{2}$
	2	4	4
	3	$\tfrac{11}{2}$	5 ←
3	1	$\tfrac{11}{2}$	$\tfrac{11}{2}$
	2	4	9
	3	$\tfrac{11}{2}$	7 ←

The policy improvement in this case was performed by means of both gains and values. The gain test selected two alternatives in each state, and the value test then decided between them. The policy that has been produced is the optimal policy that was found earlier, and so there is no need to continue the procedure because we would only repeat our earlier work.

In the preceding example we began with a two-chain policy and ended with the optimal one-chain policy. The reader should start with such policies as $\mathbf{d} = \begin{bmatrix} 1 \\ 2 \\ 3 \end{bmatrix}$ and $\mathbf{d} = \begin{bmatrix} 1 \\ 1 \\ 1 \end{bmatrix}$ to see how the optimal policy with gain 7 for all states may be reached by various routes. Note that in no case is it necessary to use the true limiting values v_i; the relative values are adequate for policy-improvement purposes.

Properties of the Iteration Cycle

We shall now show that the iteration cycle of Fig. 6.1 will lead to the policy that has a higher gain in each state than any other policy. Suppose that a policy A has been evaluated so that its gains and values are known. The policy-improvement routine will use these gains and values to produce a new policy B. We need to determine the relationship between policies A and B.

If in state i the decision was made on the basis of gains, we know that

$$\sum_{j=1}^{N} p_{ij}^B g_j^A > \sum_{j=1}^{N} p_{ij}^A g_j^A$$

where superscripts A and B are used to denote the quantities pertaining to each policy. In particular, we may define

$$\psi_i = \sum_{j=1}^{N} p_{ij}^B g_j^A - \sum_{j=1}^{N} p_{ij}^A g_j^A \tag{6.6}$$

The quantity ψ_i is greater than zero if the decision in the ith state is based on gain and is equal to zero if it is based on values. If ψ_i is equal to zero, so that a value decision is made, we know that

$$q_i^B + \sum_{j=1}^{N} p_{ij}^B v_j^A \geq q_i^A + \sum_{j=1}^{N} p_{ij}^A v_j^A$$

If we let

$$\gamma_i = q_i^B + \sum_{j=1}^{N} p_{ij}^B v_j^A - q_i^A - \sum_{j=1}^{N} p_{ij}^A v_j^A \tag{6.7}$$

then $\gamma_i \geq 0$. If both ψ_i and $\gamma_i = 0$, then the policies A and B are equivalent as far as the test quantities in state i are concerned. In such a case we would arbitrarily use the decision in state i pertaining to policy A.

The policy-evaluation equations may now be written for both policies A and B according to Eqs. 6.3 and 6.4. For policy A we have

$$g_i^A = \sum_{j=1}^N p_{ij}^A g_j^A \qquad i = 1, 2, \cdots, N \qquad (6.8)$$

$$g_i^A + v_i^A = q_i^A + \sum_{j=1}^N p_{ij}^A v_j^A \qquad i = 1, 2, \cdots, N \qquad (6.9)$$

For policy B the corresponding relations are

$$g_i^B = \sum_{j=1}^N p_{ij}^B g_j^B \qquad i = 1, 2, \cdots, N \qquad (6.10)$$

$$g_i^B + v_i^B = q_i^B + \sum_{j=1}^N p_{ij}^B v_j^B \qquad i = 1, 2, \cdots, N \qquad (6.11)$$

Subtraction of Eq. 6.8 from Eq. 6.10 yields

$$g_i^B - g_i^A = \sum_{j=1}^N p_{ij}^B g_j^B - \sum_{j=1}^N p_{ij}^A g_j^A$$

If Eq. 6.6 is used to eliminate

$$\sum_{j=1}^N p_{ij}^A g_j^A$$

and we let $g_i^\Delta = g_i^B - g_i^A$, then

$$g_i^\Delta = \psi_i + \sum_{j=1}^N p_{ij}^B g_j^\Delta \qquad i = 1, 2, \cdots, N \qquad (6.12)$$

Similarly, if Eq. 6.9 is subtracted from Eq. 6.11, we obtain

$$g_i^B - g_i^A + v_i^B - v_i^A = q_i^B - q_i^A + \sum_{j=1}^N p_{ij}^B v_j^B - \sum_{j=1}^N p_{ij}^A v_j^A$$

Equation 6.7 may be used to eliminate $q_i^B - q_i^A$. Then if we let $v_i^\Delta = v_i^B - v_i^A$, we have

$$g_i^\Delta + v_i^\Delta = \gamma_i + \sum_{j=1}^N p_{ij}^B v_j^\Delta \qquad i = 1, 2, \cdots, N \qquad (6.13)$$

We have now found that the changes in gains and values must satisfy the two sets of equations (Eqs. 6.12 and 6.13). Equations 6.13 are identical to Eqs. 6.4 except that they are written in terms of differences in gain and value rather than the absolute quantities, and γ_i appears instead of q_i. However, Eqs. 6.12 differ from Eqs. 6.3 because of the term ψ_i; otherwise, if ψ_i were zero, Eqs. 6.12 would bear the same relation to Eqs. 6.3 that Eqs. 6.13 bear to Eqs. 6.4. Let us investigate further the nature of Eqs. 6.12.

PROPERTIES OF THE ITERATION CYCLE

The policy B described by parameters $p_{ij}{}^B$ and $q_i{}^B$ may of course have many independent chains. If there are L recurrent chains in the process, then we are able to identify L groups of states with the property that if the system is started in any state within a group it will always make transitions within that group. In addition there will be an $L + 1$st group of transient states with the property that if the system is started in any state of this group it will ultimately make a transition into one of the L recurrent chains. By a renumbering of states, it is possible to write the matrix $\mathbf{P}^B$ in the form

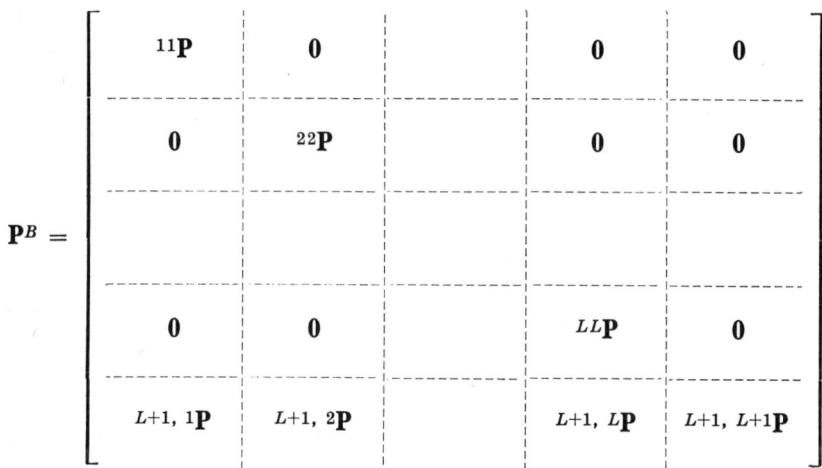

The square submatrices $^{11}\mathbf{P}$, $^{22}\mathbf{P}, \cdots, {}^{LL}\mathbf{P}$ are the transition matrices for the chains $1, 2, \cdots, L$ after the renumbering; each is itself a stochastic matrix. Submatrices of the form $^{rs}\mathbf{P}$ are composed of zero elements if $r \neq s$ and $r \neq L + 1$. The submatrix $^{L+1, L+1}\mathbf{P}$ is the matrix of transition probabilities among transient states. Some of the elements of the submatrices $^{L+1, s}\mathbf{P}$ for $s = 1, 2, \cdots, L$ must be positive.

If the same renumbering scheme is used on the vectors $\mathbf{g}^\Delta$, $\mathbf{v}^\Delta$, $\mathbf{\psi}$, $\mathbf{\gamma}$, and $\mathbf{\pi}$, we obtain a set of vectors composed of $L + 1$ subvectors; these vectors are

$$\mathbf{g}^\Delta = \begin{bmatrix} {}^1\mathbf{g}^\Delta \\ {}^2\mathbf{g}^\Delta \\ \vdots \\ {}^L\mathbf{g}^\Delta \\ {}^{L+1}\mathbf{g}^\Delta \end{bmatrix} \quad \mathbf{v}^\Delta = \begin{bmatrix} {}^1\mathbf{v}^\Delta \\ {}^2\mathbf{v}^\Delta \\ \vdots \\ {}^L\mathbf{v}^\Delta \\ {}^{L+1}\mathbf{v}^\Delta \end{bmatrix} \quad \mathbf{\psi} = \begin{bmatrix} {}^1\mathbf{\psi} \\ {}^2\mathbf{\psi} \\ \vdots \\ {}^L\mathbf{\psi} \\ {}^{L+1}\mathbf{\psi} \end{bmatrix} \quad \mathbf{\gamma} = \begin{bmatrix} {}^1\mathbf{\gamma} \\ {}^2\mathbf{\gamma} \\ \vdots \\ {}^L\mathbf{\gamma} \\ {}^{L+1}\mathbf{\gamma} \end{bmatrix}$$

$$\mathbf{\pi} = [{}^1\mathbf{\pi} \vdots {}^2\mathbf{\pi} \vdots \cdots \vdots {}^L\mathbf{\pi} \vdots {}^{L+1}\mathbf{\pi}]$$

The vector $\mathbf{\pi}$ is the state-probability vector for the L-chain process. Each subvector $^r\mathbf{\pi}$ is the limiting-state-probability vector if the system is started in a state of the rth chain; $^r\pi = {}^r\pi\,{}^{rr}\mathbf{P}$, and the sum of the components of each $^r\pi$ for $r = 1, 2, \cdots, L$ is 1. The subvector $^{L+1}\pi$ has all components zero because all states in the group $L + 1$ are transient.

Equations 6.12 and 6.13 in vector form are

$$\mathbf{g}^\Delta = \mathbf{\psi} + \mathbf{P}^B \mathbf{g}^\Delta \tag{6.14}$$

$$\mathbf{g}^\Delta + \mathbf{v}^\Delta = \mathbf{\gamma} + \mathbf{P}^B \mathbf{v}^\Delta \tag{6.15}$$

If the partitioned forms are used in Eq. 6.14, we obtain

$$^r\mathbf{g}^\Delta = {}^r\mathbf{\psi} + {}^{rr}\mathbf{P}\,{}^r\mathbf{g}^\Delta \qquad r = 1, 2, \cdots, L \tag{6.16}$$

and

$$^{L+1}\mathbf{g}^\Delta = {}^{L+1}\mathbf{\psi} + \sum_{s=1}^{L+1} {}^{L+1,s}\mathbf{P}\,{}^s\mathbf{g}^\Delta \tag{6.17}$$

Partitioning transforms Eq. 6.15 into

$$^r\mathbf{g}^\Delta + {}^r\mathbf{v}^\Delta = {}^r\mathbf{\gamma} + {}^{rr}\mathbf{P}\,{}^r\mathbf{v}^\Delta \qquad r = 1, 2, \cdots, L \tag{6.18}$$

and

$$^{L+1}\mathbf{g}^\Delta + {}^{L+1}\mathbf{v}^\Delta = {}^{L+1}\mathbf{\gamma} + \sum_{s=1}^{L+1} {}^{L+1,s}\mathbf{P}\,{}^s\mathbf{v}^\Delta \tag{6.19}$$

Suppose that Eq. 6.16 is premultiplied by $^r\pi$ so that

$$^r\pi\,{}^r\mathbf{g}^\Delta = {}^r\pi\,{}^r\mathbf{\psi} + {}^r\pi\,{}^{rr}\mathbf{P}\,{}^r\mathbf{g}^\Delta$$

Since

$$^r\pi = {}^r\pi\,{}^{rr}\mathbf{P}$$

it follows that

$$^r\pi\,{}^r\mathbf{\psi} = 0 \tag{6.20}$$

Because all states in the rth chain are recurrent, $^r\pi$ contains all positive elements. We know from our earlier discussion that all ψ_i are greater than or equal to zero. From Eq. 6.20 we see that, in any of the r groups $r = 1, 2, \cdots, L$, ψ_i must be zero. It follows that in each recurrent chain of the policy B the decision in each state must be based on *value* rather than *gain*.

Equations 6.16 thus become

$$^r\mathbf{g}^\Delta = {}^{rr}\mathbf{P}\,{}^r\mathbf{g}^\Delta \tag{6.21}$$

We know that the solution of these equations is that all $^r g_i{}^\Delta = {}^r g^\Delta$, so that all states in the rth group experience the same increase in gain as the policy is changed from A to B. If this result is used in Eq. 6.18, we find that

$$^r\mathbf{g}^\Delta = {}^r\pi\,{}^r\mathbf{\gamma} \tag{6.22}$$

PROPERTIES OF THE ITERATION CYCLE

Thus the increase in gain for each state in the rth group is equal to the vector of limiting state probabilities for the rth group times the vector of increases in the value test quantity for that group. Since, for each group $r \leqslant L$, $^r\psi_i = 0$, then $^r\gamma_i \geqslant 0$. Equation 6.22 shows that an increase in gain for each recurrent state of policy B will occur unless policies A and B are equivalent.

We have yet to determine whether or not the gain of the transient states of policy B is increased. Equation 6.17 shows that

$$(^{L+1}\mathbf{I} - {}^{L+1,L+1}\mathbf{P})^{L+1}\mathbf{g}^\Delta = {}^{L+1}\mathbf{\psi} + \sum_{s=1}^{L} {}^{L+1,s}\mathbf{P}\,{}^s\mathbf{g}^\Delta \qquad (6.23)$$

where $^{L+1}\mathbf{I}$ is an identity matrix of the same size as the number of states in the transient group $L + 1$. The change in gain of the transient states is thus given by

$$^{L+1}\mathbf{g}^\Delta = (^{L+1}\mathbf{I} - {}^{L+1,L+1}\mathbf{P})^{-1}\left(^{L+1}\mathbf{\psi} + \sum_{s=1}^{L} {}^{L+1,s}\mathbf{P}\,{}^s\mathbf{g}^\Delta\right) \qquad (6.24)$$

In the appendix it is shown that $(^{L+1}\mathbf{I} - {}^{L+1,L+1}\mathbf{P})^{-1}$ exists and has no negative elements. We know that all ψ_i are greater than or equal to zero, that some elements of the matrices $^{L+1,s}\mathbf{P}$ for $s = 1, 2, \cdots, L$ are positive and that none are negative, and that the changes in gain for the L recurrent groups cannot be negative. It follows that the change in gain for all the transient states of group $L + 1$ cannot be negative and will be positive if either or both of two conditions occur. First, the gain of a transient state will increase if its probabilistic behavior is changed so that it is more likely to run into chains of higher gain. Second, the gain of the transient state will increase if the gains of the chains into which the transient state runs are increased.

Thus we have shown that under the iteration cycle of Fig. 6.1 the gain of no state can decrease, and that the gain of some state must increase unless equivalent policies exist. We have now to show that the iteration cycle will find the policy that has highest gain in all states. Suppose that policy B has higher gain in some state than policy A, but that the iteration cycle has converged on policy A. It follows that all $\psi_i \leqslant 0$, and that, if $\psi_i = 0$, then $\gamma_i \leqslant 0$. Equation 6.22 shows that all $^r\mathbf{g}^\Delta$ are nonpositive, so that no recurrent state of policy B can have a higher gain than the same state under policy A. Since Eq. 6.24 shows that all $^{L+1}g_i^\Delta$ are nonpositive, no transient state of policy B can have a higher gain than the same state under policy A. Consequently, no state can have a higher gain under policy B than it has under policy A and still have the iteration cycle converge on policy A.

We have thus shown that the iteration cycle increases the gain of all states until it converges on the policy that has highest gain in all states, the optimal policy.

The preceding discussion may be illustrated by means of the multi-chain example of Table 6.1. Recall the case when the policy

$$\mathbf{d} = \begin{bmatrix} 3 \\ 2 \\ 1 \end{bmatrix} \qquad \mathbf{P} = \begin{bmatrix} 0 & 0 & 1 \\ 0 & 1 & 0 \\ 1 & 0 & 0 \end{bmatrix} \qquad \mathbf{q} = \begin{bmatrix} 3 \\ 4 \\ 8 \end{bmatrix}$$

changed to the policy

$$\mathbf{d} = \begin{bmatrix} 3 \\ 3 \\ 3 \end{bmatrix} \qquad \mathbf{P} = \begin{bmatrix} 0 & 0 & 1 \\ 0 & 0 & 1 \\ 0 & 0 & 1 \end{bmatrix} \qquad \mathbf{q} = \begin{bmatrix} 3 \\ 5 \\ 7 \end{bmatrix}$$

by means of the policy-improvement routine of Table 6.4. The first policy we have called policy A, the second, policy B. From Table 6.4 we see that

$$\mathbf{\psi} = \begin{bmatrix} 0 \\ \frac{3}{2} \\ 0 \end{bmatrix} \qquad \mathbf{\gamma} = \begin{bmatrix} 0 \\ 1 \\ \frac{3}{2} \end{bmatrix}$$

If the identity of states 3 and 1 is interchanged, we have

$$\mathbf{P}^B = \begin{bmatrix} 1 & 0 & 0 \\ \hline 1 & 0 & 0 \\ 1 & 0 & 0 \end{bmatrix} \qquad \mathbf{\psi} = \begin{bmatrix} 0 \\ \frac{3}{2} \\ 0 \end{bmatrix} \qquad \mathbf{\gamma} = \begin{bmatrix} \frac{3}{2} \\ 1 \\ 0 \end{bmatrix} \qquad \mathbf{g}^\Delta = \begin{bmatrix} {}^1g^\Delta \\ {}^2g^\Delta \\ {}^2g^\Delta \end{bmatrix}$$

Thus $L = 1$, there is one recurrent chain, and $^{11}\mathbf{P} = [1]$. We notice that in the new state 1 (the old state 3) the decision was based on values rather than gains. The limiting-state-probability vector for $s = 1$, $^1\boldsymbol{\pi}$, is $[1]$. Hence from Eq. 6.22

$$^1g^\Delta = \tfrac{3}{2}$$

Since

$$^{22}\mathbf{P} = \begin{bmatrix} 0 & 0 \\ 0 & 0 \end{bmatrix}$$

we see from Eq. 6.24 that

$$^2\mathbf{g}^\Delta = {}^2\boldsymbol{\psi} + {}^{21}\mathbf{P}\,{}^1g^\Delta = \begin{bmatrix} \tfrac{3}{2} \\ 0 \end{bmatrix} + \begin{bmatrix} 1 \\ 1 \end{bmatrix}[\tfrac{3}{2}] = \begin{bmatrix} 3 \\ \tfrac{3}{2} \end{bmatrix}$$

so that

$$\mathbf{g}^\Delta = \begin{bmatrix} \tfrac{3}{2} \\ 3 \\ \tfrac{3}{2} \end{bmatrix}$$

If now the renumbering of states 1 and 3 is reversed, the vector $\mathbf{g}^\Delta$ is unchanged. Hence we find that, in going from policy A to policy B, states 1 and 3 should have their gain increased by $\frac{3}{2}$, while state 2 should have its gain increased by 3. Reference to the policy-evaluation equations solved earlier for policies A and B shows that this was indeed the case.

We have seen that the multichain sequential decision process may be solved by a method extremely analogous to that for single-chain processes. However, in most practical problems knowledge of the process enables us to use the simpler single-chain approach.

7

The Sequential Decision Process with Discounting

In many economic systems the cost of money is very important. We might criticize the automobile replacement problem of Chapter 5, for example, because a dollar of expenditure in the future was given as much weight as a dollar spent at the present time. This chapter will overcome such criticisms by extending our analysis of sequential decision processes to the case in which discounting of future returns is important.

Consider a Markov process with rewards described by a transition-probability matrix **P** and a reward matrix **R**. Let the quantity β be defined as the value at the beginning of a transition interval of a unit sum received at the end of the interval. It follows that the discount factor β must be the reciprocal of 1 plus the interest rate that is applicable to the time interval required for a transition. For a nonzero interest rate, $0 \leq \beta < 1$.

Let us suppose that r_{ij} in such processes is received at the beginning of the transition from i to j. Then, if $v_i(n)$ is defined as the present value of the total expected reward for a system in state i with n transitions remaining before termination, we obtain

$$v_i(n) = \sum_{j=1}^{N} p_{ij}[r_{ij} + \beta v_j(n-1)] \qquad i = 1, 2, \cdots, N$$

$$n = 1, 2, 3, \cdots \qquad (7.1)$$

by analogy with Eqs. 2.1. Once again we may use the set of expected immediate rewards

$$q_i = \sum_{j=1}^{N} p_{ij} r_{ij}$$

to obtain for the basic recurrence relation

$$v_i(n) = q_i + \beta \sum_{j=1}^{N} p_{ij} v_j(n-1) \qquad i = 1, 2, \cdots, N$$
$$n = 1, 2, 3, \cdots \quad (7.2)$$

Equations 7.2 may also be used to analyze processes where rewards are received at the end of a transition rather than at the beginning. All that is required is that we interpret q_i as the expected present values of the rewards received in the next transition out of state i. In this way we may use Eqs. 7.2 to analyze situations where rewards are distributed in some arbitrary fashion over the transition interval.

Furthermore, Eqs. 7.2 may be used to analyze processes where discounting is not present but where there is uncertainty concerning the duration of the process. To see this, let β be defined as the probability that the process will continue to earn rewards after the next transition. Then $1 - \beta$ is the probability that the process will stop at its present stage. If the process receives no reward from stopping, then the Eqs. 7.1 and 7.2 still describe the process. It will thus not be necessary in the following to distinguish between processes with discounting and processes with indefinite duration.

Let $\mathbf{v}(n)$ be the vector of total expected rewards and $\mathbf{q}$ be the vector of expected immediate rewards. Equations 7.2 may be written as

$$\mathbf{v}(n+1) = \mathbf{q} + \beta \mathbf{P} \mathbf{v}(n) \qquad (7.3)$$

If the vector $\mathbf{v}(z)$ is defined as the z-transform of the vector $\mathbf{v}(n)$, then by the techniques of Chapter 1, we may take the z-transform of Eq. 7.3 to obtain the matrix equation

$$z^{-1}[\mathbf{v}(z) - \mathbf{v}(0)] = \frac{1}{1-z} \mathbf{q} + \beta \mathbf{P} \mathbf{v}(z)$$

Then

$$\mathbf{v}(z) - \mathbf{v}(0) = \frac{z}{1-z} \mathbf{q} + \beta z \mathbf{P} \mathbf{v}(z)$$

$$(\mathbf{I} - \beta z \mathbf{P}) \mathbf{v}(z) = \frac{z}{1-z} \mathbf{q} + \mathbf{v}(0)$$

and finally

$$\mathbf{v}(z) = \frac{z}{1-z} (\mathbf{I} - \beta z \mathbf{P})^{-1} \mathbf{q} + (\mathbf{I} - \beta z \mathbf{P})^{-1} \mathbf{v}(0) \qquad (7.4)$$

We have thus found the z-transform of $\mathbf{v}(n)$. It is now possible to find a closed-form expression for $\mathbf{v}(n)$ in any problem, so that it is not necessary to rely on the recurrence relation (Eq. 7.3).

Let us illustrate these results by applying them to the toymaker's problem of Table 3.1. Suppose that the toymaker is following the policy

$$\mathbf{d} = \begin{bmatrix} 1 \\ 1 \end{bmatrix} \qquad \mathbf{P} = \begin{bmatrix} \tfrac{1}{2} & \tfrac{1}{2} \\ \tfrac{2}{5} & \tfrac{3}{5} \end{bmatrix} \qquad \mathbf{q} = \begin{bmatrix} 6 \\ -3 \end{bmatrix}$$

He is not advertising and not conducting research. Suppose also that for each week there is a probability of $\tfrac{1}{2}$ that he will go completely out of business before the next week starts. If he goes out of business, he still receives his immediate rewards for the present week but receives no other reward. The problem as stated fits our framework with $\beta = \tfrac{1}{2}$. We shall assume that $\mathbf{v}(0) = 0$; therefore, if he does survive for all n stages his business will have no value at that time.

For this problem, Eq. 7.4 becomes

$$\mathbf{v}(z) = \frac{z}{1-z}(\mathbf{I} - \beta z \mathbf{P})^{-1}\mathbf{q}$$

or

$$\mathbf{v}(z) = \mathcal{H}(z)\mathbf{q}$$

where we consider $\mathcal{H}(z)$ to be the z-transform of a response function $\mathbf{H}(n)$. Finally, $\mathbf{v}(n) = \mathbf{H}(n)\mathbf{q}$.

We must first find

$$\mathcal{H}(z) = \frac{z}{1-z}(\mathbf{I} - \beta z \mathbf{P})^{-1}$$

Since $\beta = \tfrac{1}{2}$,

$$(\mathbf{I} - \tfrac{1}{2}z\mathbf{P}) = \begin{bmatrix} 1 - \tfrac{1}{4}z & -\tfrac{1}{4}z \\ -\tfrac{1}{5}z & 1 - \tfrac{3}{10}z \end{bmatrix}$$

and

$$(\mathbf{I} - \tfrac{1}{2}z\mathbf{P})^{-1} = \begin{bmatrix} \dfrac{1 - \tfrac{3}{10}z}{(1 - \tfrac{1}{2}z)(1 - \tfrac{1}{20}z)} & \dfrac{\tfrac{1}{4}z}{(1 - \tfrac{1}{2}z)(1 - \tfrac{1}{20}z)} \\ \dfrac{\tfrac{1}{5}z}{(1 - \tfrac{1}{2}z)(1 - \tfrac{1}{20}z)} & \dfrac{1 - \tfrac{1}{4}z}{(1 - \tfrac{1}{2}z)(1 - \tfrac{1}{20}z)} \end{bmatrix}$$

Thus

$$\mathcal{H}(z) = \begin{bmatrix} \dfrac{z(1 - \tfrac{3}{10}z)}{(1 - z)(1 - \tfrac{1}{2}z)(1 - \tfrac{1}{20}z)} & \dfrac{\tfrac{1}{4}z^2}{(1 - z)(1 - \tfrac{1}{2}z)(1 - \tfrac{1}{20}z)} \\ \dfrac{\tfrac{1}{5}z^2}{(1 - z)(1 - \tfrac{1}{2}z)(1 - \tfrac{1}{20}z)} & \dfrac{z(1 - \tfrac{1}{4}z)}{(1 - z)(1 - \tfrac{1}{2}z)(1 - \tfrac{1}{20}z)} \end{bmatrix}$$

VALUE ITERATION

By partial-fraction expansion

$$\mathcal{H}(z) = \frac{1}{1-z}\begin{bmatrix} \frac{28}{19} & \frac{10}{19} \\ \frac{8}{19} & \frac{30}{19} \end{bmatrix} + \frac{1}{1-\frac{1}{2}z}\begin{bmatrix} -\frac{8}{9} & -\frac{10}{9} \\ -\frac{8}{9} & -\frac{10}{9} \end{bmatrix}$$

$$+ \frac{1}{1-\frac{1}{20}z}\begin{bmatrix} -\frac{100}{171} & \frac{100}{171} \\ \frac{80}{171} & -\frac{80}{171} \end{bmatrix}$$

and

$$\mathbf{H}(n) = \begin{bmatrix} \frac{28}{19} & \frac{10}{19} \\ \frac{8}{19} & \frac{30}{19} \end{bmatrix} + (\tfrac{1}{2})^n \begin{bmatrix} -\frac{8}{9} & -\frac{10}{9} \\ -\frac{8}{9} & -\frac{10}{9} \end{bmatrix}$$

$$+ (\tfrac{1}{20})^n \begin{bmatrix} -\frac{100}{171} & \frac{100}{171} \\ \frac{80}{171} & -\frac{80}{171} \end{bmatrix}$$

Since $\mathbf{v}(n) = \mathbf{H}(n)\mathbf{q}$, the problem of finding $\mathbf{v}(n)$ has been solved for an arbitrary $\mathbf{q}$. For $\mathbf{q} = \begin{bmatrix} 6 \\ -3 \end{bmatrix}$

$$\mathbf{v}(n) = \begin{bmatrix} \frac{138}{19} \\ -\frac{42}{19} \end{bmatrix} + (\tfrac{1}{2})^n \begin{bmatrix} -2 \\ -2 \end{bmatrix} + (\tfrac{1}{20})^n \begin{bmatrix} -\frac{100}{19} \\ \frac{80}{19} \end{bmatrix}$$

If the toymaker is in state 1 and has n possible stages remaining, the present value of his expected rewards from the n stages is $v_1(n) = \frac{138}{19} - 2(\tfrac{1}{2})^n - \frac{100}{19}(\tfrac{1}{20})^n$. The corresponding quantity if he is in state 2 is $v_2(n) = -\frac{42}{19} - 2(\tfrac{1}{2})^n + \frac{80}{19}(\tfrac{1}{20})^n$. Note that $v_1(0) = v_2(0) = 0$, as required. For $\mathbf{v}(0) = 0$, Eqs. 7.2 show that $v_1(1) = 6$ and $v_2(1) = -3$; these results are also confirmed by our solution. The z-transform method is thus a straightforward way to find the present value of the future rewards of a process at any stage.

We note that as n becomes very large $v_1(n)$ approaches $\frac{138}{19}$ and $v_2(n)$ approaches $-\frac{42}{19}$. For a process with discounting, the expected future reward does not grow with n as it did in the no-discounting case. Indeed, the present value of future returns approaches a constant value as n becomes very large. We shall have more to say of this behavior.

The Sequential Decision Process with Discounting Solved by Value Iteration

Just as we could use the value-iteration method to solve the sequential decision process when discounting was not important, we may now use it when discounting is important. We desire to find at each stage n the alternative we should choose in each state to make $v_i(n)$, the present value of future rewards, as large as possible. By analogy with the recurrence equation (Eq. 3.3) of the no-discounting case, we obtain for the case where discounting is important the equation

$$v_i(n+1) = \max_k \left[q_i^k + \beta \sum_{j=1}^{N} p_{ij}^k v_j(n) \right] \quad (7.5)$$

In this equation $v_i(n)$ is defined as the present value of the rewards from the remaining n stages if the system is now in state i and if the optimal selection of alternatives has been performed at each stage through stage n. For each state, the alternative k that maximizes

$$q_i^k + \beta \sum_{j=1}^{N} p_{ij}^k v_j(n)$$

is used as the decision for the ith state at stage $n+1$, or $d_i(n+1)$. Since the $v_j(n)$ are known for stage n, all the quantities needed to make the test at stage $n+1$ are at hand. Once $\mathbf{v}(0)$ is specified, the procedure can be carried through to any stage desired.

Let us work the toymaker example described by Table 3.1. We shall assume that $\beta = 0.9$, so that either the toymaker has an interest rate on his operation of 11.1 per cent per week or there is a probability 0.1 that he will go out of business in each week. The interest rate is absurdly high, but it illustrates how such a problem is handled. If transitions were made once a year, such an interest rate might be more realistic.

The solution of this problem with use of Eq. 7.5 is shown in Table 7.1. Once more we assume that $v_1(0) = v_2(0) = 0$.

Table 7.1. Solution of Toymaker's Problem with Discounting Using Value Iteration

$n =$	0	1	2	3	4	...
$v_1(n)$	0	6	7.78	9.1362	10.461658	...
$v_2(n)$	0	−3	−2.03	−0.6467	0.581197	...
$d_1(n)$	—	1	2	2	2	...
$d_2(n)$	—	1	2	2	2	...

As we shall soon prove, the total expected rewards $v_i(n)$ will increase with n and approach the values $v_1(n) = 22.2$ and $v_2(n) = 12.3$ as n becomes very large. The policy of the toymaker should be to use the second alternative in each state if $n > 1$. Since we have seen how the $v_i(n)$ approach asymptotic values for large n, we might ask if there is any way we can by-pass the recurrence relation and develop a technique that will yield directly the optimal policy for the system of very long duration. The answer is that we do have such a procedure and that it is completely analogous to the policy-iteration technique used for processes without discounting. Since the concept of gain has no meaning when rewards are discounted, the optimal policy is the one that produces the highest present value in all states. We shall now describe the new forms that the value-determination operation and the policy-improvement routine assume. We shall see that the sequential decision process with discounting is as easy to solve as the completely ergodic process without discounting. We need no longer be concerned with the chain structure of the Markov process.

The Value-Determination Operation

Suppose that the system is operating under a given policy so that a given Markov process with rewards has been specified. Then the z-transform of $\mathbf{v}(n)$, the vector of present values of expected reward in n stages, is given by Eq. 7.4 as

$$\mathfrak{v}(z) = \frac{z}{1-z}(\mathbf{I} - \beta z\mathbf{P})^{-1}\mathbf{q} + (\mathbf{I} - \beta z\mathbf{P})^{-1}\mathbf{v}(0) \qquad (7.4)$$

It was shown in Chapter 1 that $(\mathbf{I} - z\mathbf{P})^{-1}$ could be written in the form $[1/(1 - z)]\mathbf{S} + \mathcal{T}(z)$, where $\mathbf{S}$ is the matrix of limiting state probabilities and $\mathcal{T}(z)$ is the transformed matrix of components that fall to zero as n becomes large. It follows that $(\mathbf{I} - \beta z\mathbf{P})^{-1}$ can be written in the form

$$(\mathbf{I} - \beta z\mathbf{P})^{-1} = \frac{1}{1 - \beta z}\mathbf{S} + \mathcal{T}(\beta z) \qquad (7.6)$$

and that $\mathcal{T}(\beta z)$ now refers to components that fall to zero even faster as n grows large. Then Eq. 7.4 becomes

$$\mathfrak{v}(z) = \frac{z}{1-z}\left[\frac{1}{1-\beta z}\mathbf{S} + \mathcal{T}(\beta z)\right]\mathbf{q} + \left[\frac{1}{1-\beta z}\mathbf{S} + \mathcal{T}(\beta z)\right]\mathbf{v}(0) \qquad (7.7)$$

Let us investigate the behavior of Eq. 7.7 for large n. The coefficient of $\mathbf{v}(0)$ represents terms that decay to zero, so that this term disappears. The coefficient of $\mathbf{q}$ represents a step component that will remain plus transient components that will vanish. By partial-fraction expansion the step component has magnitude $[1/(1 - \beta)]\mathbf{S} + \mathcal{T}(\beta)$. Thus for large n, $\mathfrak{v}(z)$ becomes $\{[1/(1 - z)][1/(1 - \beta)]\mathbf{S} + \mathcal{T}(\beta)\}\mathbf{q}$.

For large n, $\mathbf{v}(n)$ takes the form $\{[1/(1 - \beta)]\mathbf{S} + \mathcal{T}(\beta)\}\mathbf{q}$. However, $\{[1/(1 - \beta)]\mathbf{S} + \mathcal{T}(\beta)\}$ is equal to $(\mathbf{I} - \beta\mathbf{P})^{-1}$, by Eq. 7.6. Therefore, for large n, $\mathbf{v}(n)$ approaches a limit, designated $\mathbf{v}$, that is defined by

$$\mathbf{v} = (\mathbf{I} - \beta\mathbf{P})^{-1}\mathbf{q} \qquad (7.8)$$

The vector $\mathbf{v}$ may be called the vector of present values, because each of its elements v_i is the present value of an infinite number of future expected rewards discounted by the discount factor β.

We may also derive Eq. 7.8 directly from Eq. 7.3:
$$\mathbf{v}(n+1) = \mathbf{q} + \beta \mathbf{P}\mathbf{v}(n) \tag{7.3}$$
If we write $\mathbf{v}(1), \mathbf{v}(2), \mathbf{v}(3), \cdots$ in explicit form, we find
$$\mathbf{v}(1) = \mathbf{q} + \beta \mathbf{P}\mathbf{v}(0)$$
$$\mathbf{v}(2) = \mathbf{q} + \beta \mathbf{P}\mathbf{q} + \beta^2 \mathbf{P}^2 \mathbf{v}(0)$$
$$\mathbf{v}(3) = \mathbf{q} + \beta \mathbf{P}\mathbf{q} + \beta^2 \mathbf{P}^2 \mathbf{q} + \beta^3 \mathbf{P}^3 \mathbf{v}(0)$$
$$\vdots = \vdots$$

The general form of these equations is
$$\mathbf{v}(n) = \left[\sum_{j=0}^{n-1} (\beta \mathbf{P})^j\right]\mathbf{q} + \beta^n \mathbf{P}^n \mathbf{v}(0)$$

Since $0 \leqslant \beta < 1$,
$$\lim_{n \to \infty} \mathbf{v}(n) = \sum_{j=0}^{\infty} (\beta \mathbf{P})^j \mathbf{q}$$

Because $\mathbf{P}$ is a stochastic matrix, all of its eigenvalues are less than or equal to 1 in magnitude. The matrix $\beta \mathbf{P}$ therefore has eigenvalues that are strictly less than 1 in magnitude because $0 \leqslant \beta < 1$. We may thus write $\sum_{j=0}^{\infty} (\beta \mathbf{P})^j = (\mathbf{I} - \beta \mathbf{P})^{-1}$ and obtain $\lim_{n \to \infty} \mathbf{v}(n) = \mathbf{v} = (\mathbf{I} - \beta \mathbf{P})^{-1}\mathbf{q}$, or Eq. 7.8.

The present value of future rewards in each state is finite and equal to the inverse of the $(\mathbf{I} - \beta \mathbf{P})$ matrix postmultiplied by the $\mathbf{q}$ vector. Note for future reference that, since $\mathbf{P}$ is a matrix with nonnegative elements, $(\mathbf{I} - \beta \mathbf{P})^{-1} = \sum_{j=0}^{\infty} (\beta \mathbf{P})^j$ must have nonnegative elements and, moreover, must have numbers at least as great as 1 on the main diagonal. This result is understandable from physical considerations because a $\mathbf{q}$ with nonnegative elements must produce a $\mathbf{v}$ with nonnegative elements. Since no rewards are negative, no present value can be negative.

We are now in a position to describe the value determination itself. Because we are interested in the sequential decision process for large n, we may substitute the present values $v_i = \lim_{n \to \infty} v_i(n)$ for the quantities $v_i(n)$ in Eq. 7.2 to obtain the equations
$$v_i = q_i + \beta \sum_{j=1}^{N} p_{ij} v_j \qquad i = 1, 2, \cdots, N \tag{7.9}$$

For a given set of transition probabilities p_{ij} and expected immediate rewards q_i, we may use Eqs. 7.9 to solve for the present values of the process. We are interested in the present values not only because they are the quantities that we seek to maximize in the system but also because they are the key to finding the optimal policy, as we shall see when we discuss the policy-improvement routine.

Let us find the present values for $\beta = \frac{1}{2}$ of the toymaker's policy defined by

$$\mathbf{P} = \begin{bmatrix} \frac{1}{2} & \frac{1}{2} \\ \frac{2}{5} & \frac{3}{5} \end{bmatrix} \qquad \mathbf{q} = \begin{bmatrix} 6 \\ -3 \end{bmatrix}$$

Equations 7.9 yield

$$v_1 = 6 + \tfrac{1}{4}v_1 + \tfrac{1}{4}v_2 \qquad v_2 = -3 + \tfrac{1}{5}v_1 + \tfrac{3}{10}v_2$$

The solution is $v_1 = \frac{138}{19}$, $v_2 = -\frac{42}{19}$. These are the limiting values for $v_1(n)$ and $v_2(n)$ found earlier.

We shall now see how to use the present values for policy improvement.

The Policy-Improvement Routine

The optimal policy is the one that has highest present values in all states. If we had a policy that was optimal up to stage n, according to Eq 7.5 we should maximize

$$q_i^k + \beta \sum_{j=1}^{N} p_{ij}^k v_j(n)$$

with respect to all alternatives k in the ith state. Since we are now dealing only with processes that have a large number of stages, we may substitute the present value v_j for $v_j(n)$ in this expression. We must now maximize

$$q_i^k + \beta \sum_{j=1}^{N} p_{ij}^k v_j$$

with respect to all alternatives in the ith state.

Suppose that the present values for an arbitrary policy have been determined. Then a better policy, one with higher present values in every state, can be found by the following procedure, which we call the policy-improvement routine.

For each i, find the alternative k that maximizes

$$q_i^k + \beta \sum_{j=1}^{N} p_{ij}^k v_j$$

using the v_i determined for the original policy. This k now becomes the new decision in the ith state. A new policy has been determined when this procedure has been performed for every state.

The policy-improvement routine can then be combined with the value-determination operation in the iteration cycle shown in Fig. 7.1.

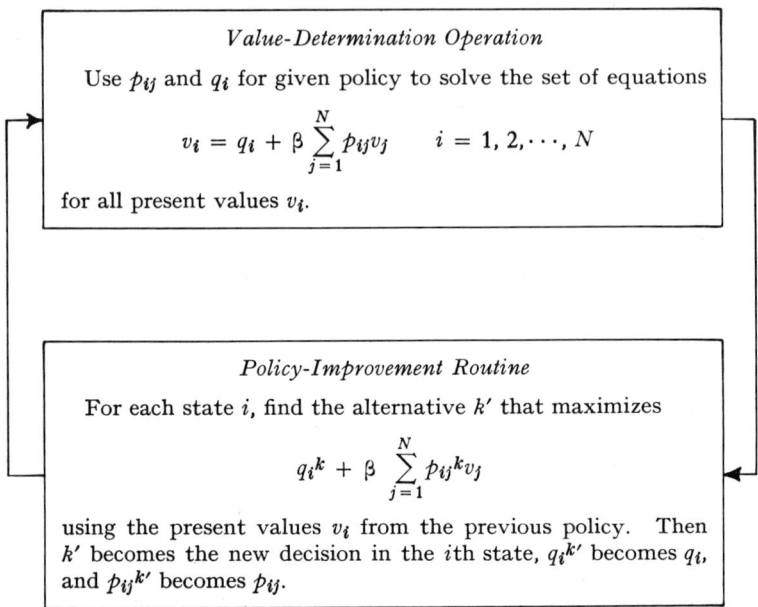

Fig. 7.1. Iteration cycle for discrete decision processes with discounting.

The iteration cycle may be entered in either box. An initial policy may be selected and the iteration begun with the value-determination operation, or an initial set of present values may be chosen and the iteration started in the policy-improvement routine. If there is no *a priori* basis for choosing a close-to-optimal policy, then it is often convenient to start the process in the policy-improvement routine with all v_i set equal to zero. The initial policy selected will then be the one that maximizes expected immediate reward, a very satisfactory starting point in most cases.

The iteration cycle will be able to make policy improvements until the policies on two successive iterations are identical. At this point it has found the optimal policy, and the problem is completed. It will be shown after the example of the next section that the policy-improvement routine must increase or leave unchanged the present values of every state and that it cannot converge on a nonoptimal policy.

An Example

Let us solve the toymaker's problem that was solved by value iteration earlier in this chapter. The data were given in Table 3.1,

AN EXAMPLE

and as before $\beta = 0.9$. We seek the policy that the toymaker should follow if his rewards are discounted and he is going to continue his business indefinitely. The optimal policy is the one that maximizes the present value of all his future rewards.

Let us choose as the initial policy the one that maximizes his expected immediate reward. This is the policy formed by the first alternative in each state, so that

$$\mathbf{d} = \begin{bmatrix} 1 \\ 1 \end{bmatrix} \qquad \mathbf{P} = \begin{bmatrix} 0.5 & 0.5 \\ 0.4 & 0.6 \end{bmatrix} \qquad \mathbf{q} = \begin{bmatrix} 6 \\ -3 \end{bmatrix}$$

Equations 7.7 of the value-determination operation yield

$$v_1 = 6 + 0.9(0.5v_1 + 0.5v_2) \qquad v_2 = -3 + 0.9(0.4v_1 + 0.6v_2)$$

The solution is $v_1 = 15.5$, $v_2 = 5.6$. The policy-improvement routine is now used as shown in Table 7.2.

Table 7.2. FIRST POLICY IMPROVEMENT FOR TOYMAKER'S PROBLEM WITH DISCOUNTING

State i	Alternative k	Value Test Quantity $q_i{}^k + \beta \sum_{j=1}^{N} p_{ij}{}^k v_j$
1	1	$6 + 0.9[0.5(15.5) + 0.5(5.6)] = 15.5$
	2	$4 + 0.9[0.8(15.5) + 0.2(5.6)] = 16.2\leftarrow$
2	1	$-3 + 0.9[0.4(15.5) + 0.6(5.6)] = 5.6$
	2	$-5 + 0.9[0.7(15.5) + 0.3(5.6)] = 6.3\leftarrow$

The second alternative in each state provides a better policy, so that now

$$\mathbf{d} = \begin{bmatrix} 2 \\ 2 \end{bmatrix} \qquad \mathbf{P} = \begin{bmatrix} 0.8 & 0.2 \\ 0.7 & 0.3 \end{bmatrix} \qquad \mathbf{q} = \begin{bmatrix} 4 \\ -5 \end{bmatrix}$$

The value-determination operation for this policy provides the equations

$$v_1 = 4 + 0.9(0.8v_1 + 0.2v_2) \qquad v_2 = -5 + 0.9(0.7v_1 + 0.3v_2)$$

From these equations we find $v_1 = 22.2$, $v_2 = 12.3$.

Notice that there has been a significant increase in present values in both states. The policy-improvement routine must be used once more as we see in Table 7.3.

The policy-improvement routine has found the same policy that it did in the previous iteration, so that this policy must be optimal. The second alternative in each state should be used if the present values of both states are to be maximized. The toymaker should advertise and do research even if faced by the 11.1 per cent interest rate per week.

Table 7.3. Second Policy Improvement for Toymaker's Problem with Discounting

State i	Alternative k	Value Test Quantity $q_i{}^k + \beta \sum_{j=1}^{N} p_{ij}{}^k v_j$
1	1	21.5
	2	22.2 ←
2	1	11.6
	2	12.3 ←

The present values of the two states under the optimal policy are 22.2 and 12.3, respectively; these present values must be higher than those of any other policy. The reader should check the policies $\mathbf{d} = \begin{bmatrix} 1 \\ 2 \end{bmatrix}$ and $\mathbf{d} = \begin{bmatrix} 2 \\ 1 \end{bmatrix}$ to make sure that this is the case.

We have seen that if the discount factor is 0.9 the optimal no-discounting policy found in Chapter 4 is still optimal for the toymaker. We shall say more about how the discount factor affects the optimal policy after we prove the properties of the iteration cycle.

Proof of the Properties of the Iteration Cycle

Consider a policy A and its successor policy B produced by the policy-improvement routine. Since B was generated from A, it follows that

$$q_i{}^B + \beta \sum_{j=1}^{N} p_{ij}{}^B v_j{}^A \geq q_i{}^A + \beta \sum_{j=1}^{N} p_{ij}{}^A v_j{}^A \qquad (7.10)$$

in every state i. We also know for the policies taken individually that

$$v_i{}^A = q_i{}^A + \beta \sum_{j=1}^{N} p_{ij}{}^A v_j{}^A \qquad (7.11)$$

$$v_i{}^B = q_i{}^B + \beta \sum_{j=1}^{N} p_{ij}{}^B v_j{}^B \qquad (7.12)$$

Let

$$\gamma_i = q_i{}^B + \beta \sum_{j=1}^{N} p_{ij}{}^B v_j{}^A - q_i{}^A - \beta \sum_{j=1}^{N} p_{ij}{}^A v_j{}^A$$

Thus γ_i is the improvement in the test quantity that the policy-improvement routine was able to achieve in the ith state; from the preceding definition, $\gamma_i \geq 0$. If we subtract Eq. 7.11 from Eq. 7.12, we obtain

$$v_i^B - v_i^A = q_i^B - q_i^A + \beta \sum_{j=1}^{N} p_{ij}^B v_j - \beta \sum_{j=1}^{N} p_{ij}^A v_j^A$$

$$= \gamma_i - \beta \sum_{j=1}^{N} p_{ij}^B v_j^A + \beta \sum_{j=1}^{N} p_{ij}^A v_j^A + \beta \sum_{j=1}^{N} p_{ij}^B v_j^B$$

$$- \beta \sum_{j=1}^{N} p_{ij}^A v_j^A$$

If $v_i^\Delta = v_i^B - v_i^A$, the increase in present value in the ith state, then

$$v_i^\Delta = \gamma_i + \beta \sum_{j=1}^{N} p_{ij}^B v_j^\Delta$$

This set of equations has the same form as our original present-value equations (Eq. 7.9), but it is written in terms of the *increase* in present values. We know that the solution in vector form is

$$\mathbf{v}^\Delta = [\mathbf{I} - \beta \mathbf{P}^B]^{-1} \mathbf{\gamma} \qquad (7.14)$$

where $\mathbf{\gamma}$ is the vector with components γ_i. It was shown earlier that $[\mathbf{I} - \beta \mathbf{P}^B]^{-1}$ has nonnegative elements and has values of at least 1 on the main diagonal. Hence, if any $\gamma_i > 0$, at least one v_i^Δ must be greater than zero, and no v_i^Δ can be less than zero. Therefore, the policy-improvement routine must increase the present values of at least one state and cannot decrease the present values of any state.

Is it possible for the routine to converge on policy A when policy B produces a higher present value in some state? No, because if the policy-improvement routine converges on A, then all $\gamma_i \leq 0$, and hence, all $v_i^\Delta \leq 0$. It follows that when the policy-improvement routine has converged on a policy no other policy can have higher present values.

The Sensitivity of the Optimal Policy to the Discount Factor

The taxicab problem discussed in Chapter 5 was solved for discount factors β ranging from 0 to 0.95 with intervals of 0.05. In this example, $1 - \beta$ might be considered to be the probability that the driver's cab will break down before his next trip. The optimal policy and present values for each situation are shown in Table 7.4. We see that, although the present values change as β increases, the optimal policy changes only as we pass certain critical values of β. More detailed calculation reveals that these critical values of β are approximately 0.13, 0.53, and 0.77. The solution for the optimal policy for different values of β is shown in Fig. 7.2. For β between 0 and 0.13, the first alternative in each state is the optimal policy; the driver should cruise in every town.

Table 7.4. Optimal Policy and Present Values for the Taxicab Problem as a Function of the Discount Factor β

Discount Factor β	Optimal Policy Decisions			Present Values		
	State 1	State 2	State 3	State 1	State 2	State 3
0	1	1	1	8.00	16.00	7.00
0.05	1	1	1	8.51	16.40	7.50
0.10	1	1	1	9.08	16.86	8.05
0.15	1	2	1	9.71	17.46	8.67
0.20	1	2	1	10.44	18.48	9.38
0.25	1	2	1	11.27	19.63	10.21
0.30	1	2	1	12.24	20.93	11.16
0.35	1	2	1	13.38	22.43	12.28
0.40	1	2	1	14.72	24.17	13.61
0.45	1	2	1	16.33	26.21	15.21
0.50	1	2	1	18.30	28.64	17.16
0.55	1	2	2	20.79	31.61	19.83
0.60	1	2	2	24.03	35.33	23.46
0.65	1	2	2	28.28	40.10	28.13
0.70	1	2	2	34.06	46.44	34.37
0.75	1	2	2	42.32	55.29	43.11
0.80	2	2	2	55.08	68.56	56.27
0.85	2	2	2	77.25	90.81	78.43
0.90	2	2	2	121.65	135.31	122.84
0.95	2	2	2	255.02	268.76	256.20

Region I Optimal Policy	Region II Optimal Policy	Region III Optimal Policy	Region IV Optimal Policy
$d = \begin{bmatrix} 1 \\ 1 \\ 1 \end{bmatrix}$	$d = \begin{bmatrix} 1 \\ 2 \\ 1 \end{bmatrix}$	$d = \begin{bmatrix} 1 \\ 2 \\ 2 \end{bmatrix}$	$d = \begin{bmatrix} 2 \\ 2 \\ 2 \end{bmatrix}$
0 0.13	0.53	0.77	1.0

β

Fig. 7.2. Optimal policy as a function of discount factor for taxicab problem.

For $\beta > 0.77$, the second alternative in each state is the optimal policy; the driver should always proceed to the nearest stand. In Region I, the policy that maximizes expected immediate reward is optimal; in Region IV, the no-discounting policy is best. An intermediate policy should be followed in Regions II and III.

The behavior first described enables us to draw several conclusions

THE AUTOMOBILE PROBLEM WITH DISCOUNTING

about the place of processes with discounting in the analysis of sequential decision processes. First, even if the no-discounting process described earlier is the preferred model of the system, the present analysis will tell us how large the discounting element of the problem must be before the no-discounting solution is no longer applicable.

Second, one criticism of a model that includes discounting is the frequent difficulty of determining what the appropriate discount rate should be. Figure 7.2 shows us that if the uncertainty about the discount rate spans only one of our regions, the same policy will be optimal, and the exact discount rate will affect only the present values.

Third, because it becomes increasingly difficult to solve the process using discounting when β is near 1, in such a situation we are better advised to solve the problem for the optimal policy without discounting.

The Automobile Problem with Discounting

The automobile replacement problem discussed in Chapter 5 was solved using a discount factor $\beta = 0.97$. This discount factor corresponds to an annual interest rate of approximately 12 per cent, a fairly realistic cost of money for the average car purchaser. Recall that the optimal no-discounting policy was found in seven iterations and that it was to buy a 3-year-old car and keep it until it was $6\frac{1}{2}$ years old. The optimal policy with discounting was found in nine iterations; it is to buy a 3-year-old car and trade it when it is $6\frac{3}{4}$ years old. The optimal no-discounting and discounting policies are very similar—if the 3 to $6\frac{1}{2}$ policy is evaluated with a discount factor $\beta = 0.97$, its present values differ negligibly from those of the 3 to $6\frac{3}{4}$ policy. This result emphasizes the point made above that the no-discounting policy is often adequate for relatively low interest rates.

The present values of the optimal policy with discounting are of interest; they are presented in Table 7.5, along with the decision in each state. Note that if we have a car less than 1 year old we should trade it for a 3-year-old car. The present values are negative because they represent a discounted stream of future costs. The present value of a 1-year-old car is $-\$4332$, while the present value of a 4-year-old car is $-\$4946$. These figures tell us that if we have a 4-year-old car we should depart from our optimal 3 to $6\frac{3}{4}$ policy if we can trade it for a 1-year-old car and pay less than $(-\$4332) - (-\$4946) = \$614$. In the no-discounting case the corresponding quantity was \$730, so that we were somewhat more willing to make such a trade when the cost of money was not important.

An interesting business opportunity is presented by Table 7.5. It appears that for a cash deposit of about \$5000 some entrepreneur

Table 7.5. OPTIMAL POLICY AND PRESENT VALUES OF AUTOMOBILE REPLACEMENT PROBLEM FOR DISCOUNT FACTOR $\beta = 0.97$

State: Age of Car in Quarterly Periods	Decision	Present Value
1	Trade for 12-period car	− $3925
2	Trade for 12-period car	− $4045
3	Trade for 12-period car	− $4155
4	Keep present car	− $4332
5	Keep present car	− $4398
6	Keep present car	− $4462
7	Keep present car	− $4523
8	Keep present car	− $4581
9	Keep present car	− $4635
10	Keep present car	− $4688
11	Keep present car	− $4738
12	Keep present car	− $4785
13	Keep present car	− $4829
14	Keep present car	− $4870
15	Keep present car	− $4909
16	Keep present car	− $4946
17	Keep present car	− $4979
18	Keep present car	− $5011
19	Keep present car	− $5041
20	Keep present car	− $5069
21	Keep present car	− $5096
22	Keep present car	− $5121
23	Keep present car	− $5145
24	Keep present car	− $5167
25	Keep present car	− $5186
26	Keep present car	− $5202
27	Trade for 12-period car	− $5215
28	Trade for 12-period car	− $5225
29	Trade for 12-period car	− $5235
30	Trade for 12-period car	− $5240
31	Trade for 12-period car	− $5245
32	Trade for 12-period car	− $5250
33	Trade for 12-period car	− $5255
34	Trade for 12-period car	− $5265
35	Trade for 12-period car	− $5270
36	Trade for 12-period car	− $5275
37	Trade for 12-period car	− $5280
38	Trade for 12-period car	− $5290
39	Trade for 12-period car	− $5298
40	Trade for 12-period car	− $5305

should be willing to supply us with the use of a car between 3 and $6\frac{3}{4}$ years old *forever*. In order to make the deal more appealing to him, we might make the deposit $6000 and allow him some profit. How unusual it would be to pay for a lifetime of car ownership in advance rather than by an unending stream of time payments and gasoline bills.

Summary

The solution of sequential decision processes is of the same order of difficulty whether or not discounting is introduced. In either case it is necessary to solve repeatedly a set of linear simultaneous equations. Each solution is followed by a set of comparisons to discover an improved policy; convergence on the optimal policy is assured. Discounting is useful when the cost of money is important or when there is uncertainty concerning the duration of the process.

8

The Continuous-Time Decision Process

In the previous chapters we have been discussing Markov processes that make state transitions at discrete, uniformly spaced intervals of time. In this chapter we shall extend our previous work to the case in which the process may make transitions at random time intervals.

The Continuous-Time Markov Process

The first problem we face is how to describe an N-state process whose time between transitions is random. Reflection shows that the significant parameters of the process must be transition rates rather than transition probabilities. Let us call a_{ij} the transition rate of a process from state i to state j, for $i \neq j$. The quantity a_{ij} is defined as follows: In a short time interval dt, a process that is now in state i will make a transition to state j with probability $a_{ij} dt$ $(i \neq j)$. The probability of two or more state transitions is of the order of $(dt)^2$ or higher and is assumed to be zero if dt is taken sufficiently small. The correspondence between this definition and the assumptions of the Poisson process should be clear. We shall consider only those processes for which the transition rates a_{ij} are constants, an assumption equivalent in the discrete-time case to the assumption that the transition probabilities do not change with time. We may now describe the continuous-time Markov process by a transition-rate matrix $\mathbf{A}$ with components a_{ij}; the diagonal elements have not yet been defined.

The probability that the system occupies state i at a time t after the start of the process is the state probability $\pi_i(t)$ by analogy with $\pi_i(n)$.

CONTINUOUS-TIME MARKOV PROCESS

We may relate the state probabilities at time t to those a short time dt later by the equations

$$\pi_j(t + dt) = \pi_j(t)\left[1 - \sum_{i \neq j} a_{ji}\, dt\right] + \sum_{i \neq j} \pi_i(t) a_{ij} dt \qquad j = 1, 2, \cdots, N \quad (8.1)$$

There are two mutually exclusive ways in which the system can occupy the state j at $t + dt$. First, it could have been in state j at time t and made no transitions during the interval dt. These events have probability $\pi_j(t)$ and $1 - \sum_{i \neq j} a_{ji}\, dt$, respectively, because we have said that the probability of multiple transitions is of order higher than dt and is negligible, and because the probability of making no transition in dt is 1 minus the probability of making a transition in dt to some state $i \neq j$. The second way the system could be in state j at $t + dt$ is to have been at state $i \neq j$ at time t and to have made a transition from i to state j during the time dt. These events have probabilities $\pi_i(t)$ and $a_{ij}\, dt$, respectively. The probabilities must be multiplied and added over all i that are not equal to j because the system could have entered j from any other state i. Thus we see how Eq. 8.1 was obtained.

Let us define the diagonal elements of the **A** matrix by

$$a_{jj} = -\sum_{i \neq j} a_{ji} \qquad (8.2)$$

If Eq. 8.2 is used in Eq. 8.1, we have

$$\pi_j(t + dt) = \pi_j(t)[1 + a_{jj}\, dt] + \sum_{i \neq j} \pi_i(t) a_{ij}\, dt$$

or

$$\pi_j(t + dt) - \pi_j(t) = \sum_{i=1}^{N} \pi_i(t) a_{ij}\, dt$$

Upon dividing both sides of this equation by dt and taking the limit as $dt \to 0$, we have

$$\frac{d}{dt}\pi_j(t) = \sum_{i=1}^{N} \pi_i(t) a_{ij} \qquad i = 1, 2, \cdots, N \quad (8.3)$$

Equations 8.3 are a set of N linear constant-coefficient differential equations that relate the state probabilities to the transition-rate matrix **A**. The initial conditions $\pi_i(0)$ for $i = 1, 2, \cdots, N$ must be specified if a solution is to be obtained.

We see that the transition-rate matrix **A** for continuous-time processes plays the same central role that the transition-probability matrix **P** played for discrete-time processes. However, we now have a set of differential equations (Eqs. 8.3) rather than a set of difference equations (Eqs. 1.2). In matrix form we may write Eqs. 8.3 as

$$\frac{d}{dt}\boldsymbol{\pi}(t) = \boldsymbol{\pi}(t)\mathbf{A} \tag{8.4}$$

where $\boldsymbol{\pi}(t)$ is the vector of state probabilities at time t. The matrix $\mathbf{A}$ is of itself interesting. The off-diagonal elements of $\mathbf{A}$ are given by the transition rates of the process. The diagonal elements of $\mathbf{A}$ are given by Eq. 8.2. As a result the rows of $\mathbf{A}$ sum to zero, or

$$\sum_{j=1}^{N} a_{ij} = 0$$

As mentioned earlier, a matrix whose rows sum to zero is called a differential matrix. As we shall see, the differential matrix $\mathbf{A}$ is a very close relative of the stochastic matrix $\mathbf{P}$.

In the following section we shall discuss the use of Laplace transforms in the solution of continuous-time Markov processes described by Eq. 8.4. We shall find that our knowledge of discrete-time Markov processes will be most helpful in our new work.

The Solution of Continuous-Time Markov Processes by Laplace Transformation

The Laplace transform of a time function $f(t)$ which is zero for $t < 0$ is defined by

$$f(s) = \int_{0}^{\infty} f(t)e^{-st}dt \tag{8.5}$$

The Laplace transform exists for any such time function that does not grow faster than exponentially. Consider, for example, the function $f(t) = e^{-at}$ for $t \geq 0$ and $f(t) = 0$ for $t < 0$. Using Eq. 8.5, we find

$$f(s) = \int_{0}^{\infty} e^{-at}e^{-st}dt = \int_{0}^{\infty} e^{-(s+a)t} = \frac{1}{s+a}$$

Table 8.1 shows some typical time functions and their corresponding Laplace transforms derived using Eq. 8.5.

The properties of Laplace transforms are widely known and are thoroughly discussed in such references as Gardner and Barnes.[2] The Laplace transform of a time function is unique; there is a one-to-one correspondence between the time function and its Laplace transformation. These transforms are particularly suited to the analysis of systems that can be described by linear constant-coefficient differential equations.

SOLUTION BY LAPLACE TRANSFORMATION

Table 8.1. LAPLACE TRANSFORM PAIRS

Time Function for $t \geq 0$	Laplace Transform
$f(t)$	$f(s)$
$f_1(t) + f_2(t)$	$f_1(s) + f_2(s)$
$kf(t)$ (k is a constant)	$kf(s)$
$\dfrac{d}{dt} f(t)$	$sf(s) - f(0)$
e^{-at}	$\dfrac{1}{s+a}$
1 (unit step)	$\dfrac{1}{s}$
te^{-at}	$\dfrac{1}{(s+a)^2}$
t (unit ramp)	$\dfrac{1}{s^2}$
$e^{-at} f(t)$	$f(s+a)$

The continuous-time Markov process is described by Eq. 8.4, so we should expect Laplace transformations to be useful in the solution of such a process. Let us designate by $\Pi(s)$ the Laplace transform of the state-probability vector $\pi(t)$. The Laplace transform of any matrix of time functions is the matrix of the Laplace transforms of the individual time functions. If we take the Laplace transform of Eq. 8.4, we obtain

$$s\Pi(s) - \pi(0) = \Pi(s)A$$

or

$$\Pi(s)(sI - A) = \pi(0)$$

where I is the identity matrix. Finally, we have

$$\Pi(s) = \pi(0)(sI - A)^{-1} \qquad (8.6)$$

The Laplace transform of the state-probability vector is thus the initial-state-probability vector postmultiplied by the inverse of the matrix $(sI - A)$. The matrix $(sI - A)^{-1}$ is the continuous-process counterpart of the matrix $(I - zP)^{-1}$. We shall find that it has properties analogous to those of $(I - zP)^{-1}$ and that it constitutes a complete solution of the continuous-time Markov process.

By inspection, we see that the solution of Eq. 8.4 is

$$\pi(t) = \pi(0)e^{At} \qquad (8.7)$$

where the matrix function e^{At} is to be interpreted as the exponential series

$$I + tA + \frac{t^2}{2!} A^2 + \frac{t^3}{3!} A^3 + \cdots$$

which will converge to e^{At}. For discrete processes, Eqs. 1.4 yielded

$$\pi(n) = \pi(0)\mathbf{P}^n \qquad n = 0, 1, 2, \cdots \qquad (1.4)$$

Suppose that we wish to find the matrix $\mathbf{A}$ for the continuous-time process that will have the same state probabilities as the discrete process described by $\mathbf{P}$ at the times $t = 0, 1, 2, \cdots$, where a unit of time is defined as the time for one transition of the discrete process. Then, by comparison of Eqs. 8.7 and 1.4 when $t = n$, we see that

$$e^{\mathbf{A}} = \mathbf{P}$$

or

$$\mathbf{A} = \ln \mathbf{P} \qquad (8.8)$$

Recall the toymaker's initial policy, for which the transition-probability matrix was

$$\mathbf{P} = \begin{bmatrix} \frac{1}{2} & \frac{1}{2} \\ \frac{2}{5} & \frac{3}{5} \end{bmatrix}$$

Suppose that we should like to find the continuous process that will have the same state probabilities at the end of each week for an arbitrary starting position. Then we would have to solve Eq. 8.8 to find the matrix $\mathbf{A}$. Methods for accomplishing this exist,[4] and if we apply them to the toymaker's $\mathbf{P}$ we find

$$\mathbf{A} = \frac{\ln 10}{9} \begin{bmatrix} -5 & 5 \\ 4 & -4 \end{bmatrix}$$

Since the constant factor $(\ln 10)/9$ is annoying from the point of view of calculation, we may as well solve a problem that is analogous to the toymaker's problem but that is not encumbered by the constants necessary for complete correspondence in the sense just described. We shall let $\mathbf{A}$ be simply

$$\mathbf{A} = \begin{bmatrix} -5 & 5 \\ 4 & -4 \end{bmatrix} \qquad (8.9)$$

Since we are abandoning complete correspondence, we may as well treat ourselves to a change in problem interpretations at the same time. We shall call this new problem "the foreman's dilemma." A machine-shop foreman has a cantankerous machine that may be either working (state 1) or not working (state 2). If it is working, there is a probability $5\,dt$ that it will break down in a short interval dt; if it is not working, there is a probability $4\,dt$ that it will be repaired in dt. We thus obtain the transition-rate matrix (Eq. 8.9). The assumptions regarding breakdown and repair are equivalent to saying that the operating time between breakdowns is exponentially distributed with mean $\frac{1}{5}$, while

SOLUTION BY LAPLACE TRANSFORMATION 97

the time required for repair is exponentially distributed with mean $\frac{1}{4}$. If we take 1 hour as our time unit, we expect a breakdown to occur after 12 minutes of operation, and we expect a repair to take 15 minutes. The standard deviation of operating and repair times is also equal to 12 and 15, respectively.

For the foreman's problem we would like to find, for example, the probability that the machine will be operating at time t if it is operating when $t = 0$. To answer such a question, we must apply the analysis of Eq. 8.6 to the matrix (Eq. 8.9). We find

$$s\mathbf{I} - \mathbf{A} = \begin{bmatrix} s+5 & -5 \\ -4 & s+4 \end{bmatrix}$$

$$(s\mathbf{I} - \mathbf{A})^{-1} = \begin{bmatrix} \dfrac{s+4}{s(s+9)} & \dfrac{5}{s(s+9)} \\ \dfrac{4}{s(s+9)} & \dfrac{s+5}{s(s+9)} \end{bmatrix}$$

Partial-fraction expansion permits

$$(s\mathbf{I} - \mathbf{A})^{-1} = \begin{bmatrix} \dfrac{\frac{4}{9}}{s} + \dfrac{\frac{5}{9}}{s+9} & \dfrac{\frac{5}{9}}{s} + \dfrac{-\frac{5}{9}}{s+9} \\ \dfrac{\frac{4}{9}}{s} + \dfrac{-\frac{4}{9}}{s+9} & \dfrac{\frac{5}{9}}{s} + \dfrac{\frac{4}{9}}{s+9} \end{bmatrix}$$

or

$$(s\mathbf{I} - \mathbf{A})^{-1} = \frac{1}{s}\begin{bmatrix} \frac{4}{9} & \frac{5}{9} \\ \frac{4}{9} & \frac{5}{9} \end{bmatrix} + \frac{1}{s+9}\begin{bmatrix} \frac{5}{9} & -\frac{5}{9} \\ -\frac{4}{9} & \frac{4}{9} \end{bmatrix}$$

Let the matrix $\mathbf{H}(t)$ be the inverse transform of $(s\mathbf{I} - \mathbf{A})^{-1}$. Then Eq. 8.6 becomes by means of inverse transformation

$$\boldsymbol{\pi}(t) = \boldsymbol{\pi}(0)\mathbf{H}(t) \qquad (8.10)$$

By comparing Eqs. 8.7 and 8.10, we see that $\mathbf{H}(t)$ is a closed-form expression for $e^{\mathbf{A}t}$.

For the foreman example,

$$\mathbf{H}(t) = \begin{bmatrix} \frac{4}{9} & \frac{5}{9} \\ \frac{4}{9} & \frac{5}{9} \end{bmatrix} + e^{-9t}\begin{bmatrix} \frac{5}{9} & -\frac{5}{9} \\ -\frac{4}{9} & \frac{4}{9} \end{bmatrix}$$

The state-probability vector $\boldsymbol{\pi}(t)$ may be obtained by postmultiplying the initial-state-probability vector $\boldsymbol{\pi}(0)$ by the matrix $\mathbf{H}(t)$. If the machine is operating at $t = 0$, so that $\boldsymbol{\pi}(0) = [1 \ \ 0]$, then $\boldsymbol{\pi}(t) = [\frac{4}{9} \ \ \frac{5}{9}] + e^{-9t}[\frac{5}{9} \ \ -\frac{5}{9}]$ or $\pi_1(t) = \frac{4}{9} + \frac{5}{9}e^{-9t}$, $\pi_2(t) = \frac{5}{9} - \frac{5}{9}e^{-9t}$. Both $\pi_1(t)$ and $\pi_2(t)$ have a constant term plus an exponentially decaying term. The constant term represents the limiting state probability as t becomes very large. Thus the probability that the machine is operating, $\pi_1(t)$, falls exponentially from 1 to $\tfrac{4}{9}$ as t increases. The time constant for this exponential decay is $\tfrac{1}{9}$.

Similarly, if the machine is not working at $t = 0$, $\pi(0) = [0 \ 1]$, and $\pi(t) = [\tfrac{4}{9} \ \tfrac{5}{9}] + e^{-9t}[-\tfrac{4}{9} \ \tfrac{4}{9}]$, so that $\pi_1(t) = \tfrac{4}{9} - \tfrac{4}{9}e^{-9t}$, $\pi_2(t) = \tfrac{5}{9} + \tfrac{4}{9}e^{-9t}$. Note that the probability that the machine is working rises exponentially from 0 to its steady-state value of $\tfrac{4}{9}$ as t becomes large. The limiting state probabilities of the process are $\tfrac{4}{9}$ and $\tfrac{5}{9}$ for states 1 and 2, respectively. They are independent of the state of the system at $t = 0$.

The similarity between the discrete-time and continuous-time Markov processes is now apparent. Both have limiting state probabilities and transient components of probability. The transients in the discrete case were geometric; in the continuous case they are exponential. The matrix $(s\mathbf{I} - \mathbf{A})^{-1}$ will always have one term of the form $1/s$ times a stochastic matrix $\mathbf{S}$. This is true because s is a factor of the determinant of $(s\mathbf{I} - \mathbf{A})$; a differential matrix always has one characteristic value that equals zero. The stochastic matrix $\mathbf{S}$ is the matrix of limiting-state-probability vectors, as it was in the discrete case. The ith row of $\mathbf{S}$ is the limiting-state-probability vector of the process if it is started in the ith state. The remarks concerning recurrent chains still apply in the continuous-time process.

The remaining terms of $(s\mathbf{I} - \mathbf{A})^{-1}$ represent transient components of the form e^{-at}, te^{-at}, and so on, that vanish for large t. The matrices multiplying these components are themselves differential matrices. We may call $\mathscr{T}(s)$ the transient part of $(s\mathbf{I} - \mathbf{A})^{-1}$ and write

$$(s\mathbf{I} - \mathbf{A})^{-1} = \frac{1}{s}\mathbf{S} + \mathscr{T}(s) \tag{8.11}$$

or

$$\mathbf{H}(t) = \mathbf{S} + \mathbf{T}(t) \tag{8.12}$$

where $\mathbf{S}$ is the stochastic matrix of limiting state probabilities and $\mathbf{T}(t)$ contains the transient components of probability. For the foreman's problem

$$\mathbf{S} = \begin{bmatrix} \tfrac{4}{9} & \tfrac{5}{9} \\ \tfrac{4}{9} & \tfrac{5}{9} \end{bmatrix} \qquad \mathbf{T}(t) = e^{-9t}\begin{bmatrix} \tfrac{5}{9} & -\tfrac{5}{9} \\ -\tfrac{4}{9} & \tfrac{4}{9} \end{bmatrix}$$

The rows of $\mathbf{S}$ are identical because the process is completely ergodic.

It is not necessary to find $(s\mathbf{I} - \mathbf{A})^{-1}$ if only the limiting state probabilities are required. Suppose that the process is completely ergodic. Since the limiting state probabilities are constants, we know that

$d\pi(t)/dt = 0$ for large t. If we denote the limiting-state-probability vector by π, then Eq. 8.4 becomes

$$0 = \pi A \qquad (8.13)$$

This set of simultaneous equations plus the requirement

$$\sum_{i=1}^{N} \pi_i = 1 \qquad (8.14)$$

is sufficient to determine the limiting state probabilities. For the matrix A (Eq. 8.9) we have from Eq. 8.13

$$-5\pi_1 + 4\pi_2 = 0 \qquad 5\pi_1 - 4\pi_2 = 0$$

and from Eq. 8.14

$$\pi_1 + \pi_2 = 1$$

The solution of these equations is $\pi_1 = \frac{4}{9}$, $\pi_2 = \frac{5}{9}$, in accordance with our earlier results.

The Continuous-Time Markov Process with Rewards

Just as the notion of continuous time made us think in terms of transition rates rather than transition probabilities, so we must redefine the concept of reward. Let us suppose that the system earns a reward at the rate of r_{ii} dollars per unit time during all the time that it occupies state i. Suppose further that when the system makes a transition from state i to state j ($i \neq j$) it receives a reward of r_{ij} dollars. (Note that r_{ii} and r_{ij} have different dimensions.) It is not necessary that the system earn according to both reward rates and transition rewards, but these definitions give us generality.

We are interested in the expected earnings of the system if it operates for a time t with a given initial condition. If we let $v_i(t)$ be the expected total reward that the system will earn in a time t if it starts in state i, then we can relate the total expected reward in a time $t + dt$, $v_i(t + dt)$, to $v_i(t)$ by Eq. 8.15. Here dt represents, as before, a very short time interval:

$$v_i(t + dt) = \left(1 - \sum_{j \neq i} a_{ij}\, dt\right)[r_{ii}\, dt + v_i(t)] + \sum_{j \neq i} a_{ij}\, dt[r_{ij} + v_j(t)] \qquad (8.15)$$

Equation 8.15 may be interpreted as follows. During the time interval dt the system may remain in state i or make a transition to some other state j. If it remains in state i for a time dt, it will earn a reward $r_{ii}\, dt$ plus the expected reward that it will earn in the remaining t units of time, $v_i(t)$. The probability that it remains in state i for a time dt is 1 minus the probability that it makes a transition in dt, or

$1 - \sum_{j \neq i} a_{ij} \, dt$. On the other hand, the system may make a transition to some state $j \neq i$ during the time interval dt with probability $a_{ij} \, dt$. In this case the system would receive the reward r_{ij} plus the expected reward to be made if it starts in state j with time t remaining, $v_j(t)$. The product of probability and reward must then be summed over all states $j \neq i$ to obtain the total contribution to the expected values.

Using Eq. 8.2, we may write Eq. 8.15 as

$$v_i(t + dt) = (1 + a_{ii} \, dt)[r_{ii} \, dt + v_i(t)] + \sum_{j \neq i} a_{ij} \, dt[r_{ij} + v_j(t)]$$

or

$$v_i(t + dt) = r_{ii} \, dt + v_i(t) + a_{ii} v_i(t) \, dt + \sum_{j \neq i} a_{ij} r_{ij} \, dt + \sum_{j \neq i} a_{ij} v_j(t) \, dt$$

where terms of higher order than dt have been neglected. Finally, if we subtract $v_i(t)$ from both sides of the equation and divide by dt, we have

$$\frac{v_i(t + dt) - v_i(t)}{dt} = r_{ii} + \sum_{j \neq i} a_{ij} r_{ij} + \sum_{j=1}^{N} a_{ij} v_j(t)$$

If we take the limit as $dt \to 0$, we obtain

$$\frac{d}{dt} v_i(t) = r_{ii} + \sum_{j \neq i} a_{ij} r_{ij} + \sum_{j=1}^{N} a_{ij} v_j(t) \qquad i = 1, 2, \cdots, N$$

We now have a set of N linear constant-coefficient differential equations that completely define $v_i(t)$ when the $v_i(0)$ are known. Let us define a quantity q_i as the "earning rate" of the system where

$$q_i = r_{ii} + \sum_{j \neq i} a_{ij} r_{ij} \tag{8.16}$$

In the foreman's problem, for example, the machine might have earning rates $q_1 = 6$, $q_2 = -3$. These earning rates could be composed of many different combinations of reward rates and transition rewards. Thus, if the reward rate in state 1 is \$6 per unit time, the reward rate in state 2 is $-\$3$ per unit time, and there is no reward associated with transitions, then $r_{11} = 6$, $r_{22} = -3$, $r_{12} = r_{21} = 0$, and we obtain the earning rates just mentioned. In a later section we consider the q_i to be obtained partly from transition rewards, but for the moment it makes no difference.

With use of the definition of earning rate, our equations become

$$\frac{d}{dt} v_i(t) = q_i + \sum_{j=1}^{N} a_{ij} v_j(t) \qquad i = 1, 2, \cdots, N \tag{8.17}$$

CONTINUOUS-TIME MARKOV PROCESS WITH REWARDS

Equations 8.17 are a set of linear, constant-coefficient differential equations that relate the total reward in time t from a start in state i to the quantities q_i and a_{ij}. If $\mathbf{v}(t)$ is designated as the column vector with elements $v_i(t)$, the total expected rewards, and if $\mathbf{q}$ is designated as the earning-rate vector with components q_i, then Eqs. 8.17 can be written in matrix form as

$$\frac{d}{dt}\mathbf{v}(t) = \mathbf{q} + \mathbf{A}\mathbf{v}(t) \tag{8.18}$$

To obtain a solution to Eq. 8.18, we must of course specify $\mathbf{v}(0)$. Since Eq. 8.18 is a linear constant-coefficient differential equation, the Laplace transform should provide a useful method of solution. If the Laplace transform of Eq. 8.18 is taken according to Table 8.1, we have

$$s\mathbf{v}(s) - \mathbf{v}(0) = \frac{1}{s}\mathbf{q} + \mathbf{A}\mathbf{v}(s)$$

or

$$(s\mathbf{I} - \mathbf{A})\mathbf{v}(s) = \frac{1}{s}\mathbf{q} + \mathbf{v}(0)$$

and finally

$$\mathbf{v}(s) = \frac{1}{s}(s\mathbf{I} - \mathbf{A})^{-1}\mathbf{q} + (s\mathbf{I} - \mathbf{A})^{-1}\mathbf{v}(0) \tag{8.19}$$

Thus we find that Eq. 8.19 relates $\mathbf{v}(s)$, the Laplace transform of $\mathbf{v}(t)$, to $(s\mathbf{I} - \mathbf{A})^{-1}$, the earning-rate vector $\mathbf{q}$ and the termination-reward vector $\mathbf{v}(0)$, respectively. The reward vector $\mathbf{v}(t)$ may be found by inverse transformation of Eq. 8.19.

Let us apply the result (Eq. 8.19) to the foreman's problem. The transition-rate matrix and reward vector are

$$\mathbf{A} = \begin{bmatrix} -5 & 5 \\ 4 & -4 \end{bmatrix} \qquad \mathbf{q} = \begin{bmatrix} 6 \\ -3 \end{bmatrix}$$

We shall assume that the machine will be thrown away at $t = 0$, so that $v_1(0) = v_2(0) = 0$. We found earlier that for this problem

$$(s\mathbf{I} - \mathbf{A})^{-1} = \begin{bmatrix} \dfrac{s+4}{s(s+9)} & \dfrac{5}{s(s+9)} \\ \dfrac{4}{s(s+9)} & \dfrac{s+5}{s(s+9)} \end{bmatrix}$$

THE CONTINUOUS-TIME DECISION PROCESS

To use Eq. 8.19, we must find $(1/s)(s\mathbf{I} - \mathbf{A})^{-1}$. This is

$$\frac{1}{s}(s\mathbf{I} - \mathbf{A})^{-1} = \begin{bmatrix} \dfrac{s+4}{s^2(s+9)} & \dfrac{5}{s^2(s+9)} \\ \dfrac{4}{s^2(s+9)} & \dfrac{s+5}{s^2(s+9)} \end{bmatrix}$$

Using partial-fraction expansion, we obtain

$$\frac{1}{s}(s\mathbf{I} - \mathbf{A})^{-1} = \begin{bmatrix} \dfrac{\frac{4}{9}}{s^2} + \dfrac{\frac{5}{81}}{s} + \dfrac{-\frac{5}{81}}{s+9} & \dfrac{\frac{5}{9}}{s^2} + \dfrac{-\frac{5}{81}}{s} + \dfrac{\frac{5}{81}}{s+9} \\ \dfrac{\frac{4}{9}}{s^2} + \dfrac{-\frac{4}{81}}{s} + \dfrac{\frac{4}{81}}{s+9} & \dfrac{\frac{5}{9}}{s^2} + \dfrac{\frac{4}{81}}{s} + \dfrac{-\frac{4}{81}}{s+9} \end{bmatrix}$$

$$= \frac{1}{s^2}\begin{bmatrix} \frac{4}{9} & \frac{5}{9} \\ \frac{4}{9} & \frac{5}{9} \end{bmatrix} + \frac{1}{s}\begin{bmatrix} \frac{5}{81} & -\frac{5}{81} \\ -\frac{4}{81} & \frac{4}{81} \end{bmatrix} + \frac{1}{s+9}\begin{bmatrix} -\frac{5}{81} & \frac{5}{81} \\ \frac{4}{81} & -\frac{4}{81} \end{bmatrix}$$

Thus, since $\mathbf{V}(s) = (1/s)(s\mathbf{I} - \mathbf{A})^{-1}\mathbf{q}$, by inverse transformation

$$\mathbf{v}(t) = \left\{ t\begin{bmatrix} \frac{4}{9} & \frac{5}{9} \\ \frac{4}{9} & \frac{5}{9} \end{bmatrix} + \begin{bmatrix} \frac{5}{81} & -\frac{5}{81} \\ -\frac{4}{81} & \frac{4}{81} \end{bmatrix} + e^{-9t}\begin{bmatrix} -\frac{5}{81} & \frac{5}{81} \\ \frac{4}{81} & -\frac{4}{81} \end{bmatrix} \right\}\begin{bmatrix} 6 \\ -3 \end{bmatrix}$$

or

$$\mathbf{v}(t) = t\begin{bmatrix} 1 \\ 1 \end{bmatrix} + \begin{bmatrix} \frac{5}{9} \\ -\frac{4}{9} \end{bmatrix} + e^{-9t}\begin{bmatrix} -\frac{5}{9} \\ \frac{4}{9} \end{bmatrix}$$

The total expected reward in time t if the system is started in state 1 is thus

$$v_1(t) = t + \tfrac{5}{9} - \tfrac{5}{9}e^{-9t}$$

and if started in state 2 is

$$v_2(t) = t - \tfrac{4}{9} + \tfrac{4}{9}e^{-9t}$$

Note that regardless of the starting state the machine will earn, on the average, $1 per unit time when t is large because the coefficient of t in both $v_1(t)$ and $v_2(t)$ is 1. The average reward per unit time for a system is called the gain of the system by analogy with the discrete-time case. As before, the gain will depend upon the starting state if the system is not completely ergodic. We also see that for large t, $v_1(t)$ and $v_2(t)$ may be written in the form $v_i(t) = g_i t + v_i$; in the above case, $v_1 = \tfrac{5}{9}$, $v_2 = -\tfrac{4}{9}$. Let us prove that this relation holds for a general continuous-time Markov process.

Equation 8.19 is

$$\mathbf{v}(s) = \frac{1}{s}(s\mathbf{I} - \mathbf{A})^{-1}\mathbf{q} + (s\mathbf{I} - \mathbf{A})^{-1}\mathbf{v}(0) \tag{8.19}$$

CONTINUOUS-TIME MARKOV PROCESS WITH REWARDS 103

We know from Eq. 8.11 that

$$(s\mathbf{I} - \mathbf{A})^{-1} = \frac{1}{s}\mathbf{S} + \mathcal{T}(s) \tag{8.11}$$

where $\mathbf{S}$ is the matrix of limiting state probabilities and $\mathcal{T}(s)$ consists of transforms of purely transient components. If Eq. 8.11 is substituted into Eq. 8.19, we have

$$\mathbf{v}(s) = \frac{1}{s}\left[\frac{1}{s}\mathbf{S} + \mathcal{T}(s)\right]\mathbf{q} + \left[\frac{1}{s}\mathbf{S} + \mathcal{T}(s)\right]\mathbf{v}(0)$$

or

$$\mathbf{v}(s) = \frac{1}{s^2}\mathbf{S}\mathbf{q} + \frac{1}{s}\mathcal{T}(s)\mathbf{q} + \frac{1}{s}\mathbf{S}\mathbf{v}(0) + \mathcal{T}(s)\mathbf{v}(0) \tag{8.20}$$

We shall investigate the behavior of $\mathbf{v}(t)$ for large t by determining the behavior of each component of Eq. 8.20. The term $(1/s^2)\mathbf{S}\mathbf{q}$ represents a ramp of magnitude $\mathbf{S}\mathbf{q}$. The second term $(1/s)\mathcal{T}(s)\mathbf{q}$ refers to both step and exponential transient components. The transient components vanish for large t; the step component has magnitude $\mathcal{T}(0)\mathbf{q}$. The term $(1/s)\mathbf{S}\mathbf{v}(0)$ represents a step of magnitude $\mathbf{S}\mathbf{v}(0)$; the term $\mathcal{T}(s)\mathbf{v}(0)$ refers to transient components that vanish for large t.

Thus when t is large, $\mathbf{v}(t)$ has the form

$$\mathbf{v}(t) = t\mathbf{S}\mathbf{q} + \mathcal{T}(0)\mathbf{q} + \mathbf{S}\mathbf{v}(0) \tag{8.21}$$

If a vector $\mathbf{g}$ of state gains g_i is defined by

$$\mathbf{g} = \mathbf{S}\mathbf{q} \tag{8.22}$$

and if a vector $\mathbf{v}$ with components v_i is defined by

$$\mathbf{v} = \mathcal{T}(0)\mathbf{q} + \mathbf{S}\mathbf{v}(0) \tag{8.23}$$

then Eq. 8.21 becomes

$$\mathbf{v}(t) = t\mathbf{g} + \mathbf{v} \qquad \text{for large } t \tag{8.24}$$

or

$$v_i(t) = tg_i + v_i \qquad \text{for large } t \tag{8.25}$$

We see that the total expected reward in time t for a continuous-time system started in state i has the same form as the corresponding quantity in the discrete-time case (Eq. 2.15) except that n has been replaced by t. For the foreman's problem,

$$(s\mathbf{I} - \mathbf{A})^{-1} = \frac{1}{s}\begin{bmatrix} \frac{4}{9} & \frac{5}{9} \\ \frac{4}{9} & \frac{5}{9} \end{bmatrix} + \frac{1}{s+9}\begin{bmatrix} \frac{5}{9} & -\frac{5}{9} \\ -\frac{4}{9} & \frac{4}{9} \end{bmatrix}$$

$$= \frac{1}{s}\mathbf{S} + \mathcal{T}(s)$$

so that

$$\mathbf{S} = \begin{bmatrix} \frac{4}{9} & \frac{5}{9} \\ \frac{4}{9} & \frac{5}{9} \end{bmatrix} \qquad \mathcal{T}(0) = \begin{bmatrix} \frac{5}{81} & -\frac{5}{81} \\ -\frac{4}{81} & \frac{4}{81} \end{bmatrix}$$

In addition, $\mathbf{q} = \begin{bmatrix} 6 \\ -3 \end{bmatrix}$. From Eq. 8.22, we have $\mathbf{g} = \mathbf{Sq} = \begin{bmatrix} 1 \\ 1 \end{bmatrix}$, and from Eq. 8.23, since $\mathbf{v}(0) = 0$, we have $\mathbf{v} = \mathcal{T}(0)\mathbf{q} = \begin{bmatrix} \frac{5}{9} \\ -\frac{4}{9} \end{bmatrix}$.

Therefore by Eq. 8.25, it follows that for large t we may write $v_1(t)$ and $v_2(t)$ in the form

$$v_1(t) = t + \tfrac{5}{9} \qquad v_2(t) = t - \tfrac{4}{9}$$

These expressions agree with those found previously.

We have now completed our analysis of the continuous-time Markov process with given earning rates in each state. The reader should compare the results of the foreman's problem analyzed in this section with those found for the analogous toymaker's problem in order to understand clearly the similarities and differences of discrete and continuous-time Markov processes. We shall now turn to a study of the continuous-time decision problem.

The Continuous-Time Decision Problem

Suppose that our machine shop foreman has to decide upon a maintenance and repair policy for the machinery. When the system is in state 1, or working, the foreman must decide what kind of maintenance he will use. Let us suppose that if he uses normal maintenance procedures the facility will earn \$6 per unit time and will have a probability $5\,dt$ of breaking down in a short time dt. Note that this is equivalent to saying that the length of operating intervals of the machine is exponentially distributed with mean $\tfrac{1}{5}$.

The foreman also has the option of a more expensive maintenance procedure that will reduce earnings to \$4 per unit time but will also reduce the probability of a breakdown in dt to $2\,dt$. Under neither of these maintenance schemes is there a cost associated with the breakdown *per se*. If we number the two alternatives in state 1 as 1 and 2, respectively, then we have for the first alternative

$$a_{12}{}^1 = 5 \qquad r_{11}{}^1 = 6 \qquad r_{12}{}^1 = 0$$

and for the second alternative

$$a_{12}{}^2 = 2 \qquad r_{11}{}^2 = 4 \qquad r_{12}{}^2 = 0$$

Finally, we obtain by using Eq. 8.16 that

$$q_1{}^1 = 6 \quad \text{and} \quad q_1{}^2 = 4$$

CONTINUOUS-TIME DECISION PROBLEM

Now we must consider what can happen when the machinery is not working and the system occupies state 2. Let us suppose that the foreman also has two alternatives in this state. First, he may have the repair work done by his own men. For this alternative the repair will cost $1 per unit time that the men are working, plus $0.50 fixed charge per breakdown, and there is a probability $4\,dt$ that the machine will be repaired in a short time dt (repair time is exponential with mean $\frac{1}{4}$). The parameters of this alternative are thus

$$a_{21}{}^1 = 4 \qquad r_{22}{}^1 = -1 \qquad r_{21}{}^1 = -0.5$$

and using Eq. 8.16, we have

$$q_2{}^1 = -1 + (4)(-0.5) = -3$$

The second alternative for the supervisor when the machine is not working is to use an outside repair firm. For this alternative the fixed charge per breakdown is the same, $0.50. However, these men will cost $1.50 per unit time, but will increase the probability of a repair in dt to $7\,dt$. Thus, for this alternative

$$a_{21}{}^2 = 7 \qquad r_{22}{}^2 = -1.5 \qquad r_{21}{}^2 = -0.5$$

and

$$q_2{}^2 = -1.5 + 7(-0.5) = -5$$

The foreman must decide which alternative to use in each state in order to maximize his profits in the long run. The data for the problem are summarized in Table 8.2.

Table 8.2. THE FOREMAN'S DILEMMA

State i	Alternative k	Transition Rate $a_{i1}{}^k$	Transition Rate $a_{i2}{}^k$	Earning Rate $q_i{}^k$
1 (Facility operating)	1 (Normal maintenance)	−5	5	6
	2 (Expensive maintenance)	−2	2	4
2 (Facility out of order)	1 (Inside repair)	4	−4	−3
	2 (Outside repair)	7	−7	−5

The concepts of alternative, decision, and policy carry over from the discrete situation. Since each of the four possible policies contained in Table 8.2 represents a completely ergodic process, each has a unique gain that is independent of the starting state of the system. The foreman would like to find the policy that has highest gain; this is the optimal policy.

One way to find the optimal policy is to find the gain for each of the four policies and see which gain is largest. Although this is feasible for small problems, it is not feasible for problems that have many states and many alternatives in each state.

Note also that the value-iteration method available for discrete-time processes is no longer practical in the continuous-time case. It is not possible to use simple recursive relations that will lead ultimately to the optimal policy because we are now dealing with differential rather than difference equations.

A policy-iteration method has been developed for the solution of the long-duration continuous-time decision problem. It is in all major respects completely analogous to the procedure used in discrete-time processes. As before, the heart of the procedure is an iteration cycle composed of a value-determination operation and a policy-improvement routine. We shall now discuss each section in detail.

The Value-Determination Operation

For a given policy the total expected reward of the system in time t is governed by Eqs. 8.17

$$\frac{d}{dt} v_i(t) = q_i + \sum_{j=1}^{N} a_{ij} v_j(t) \qquad i = 1, 2, \cdots, N \qquad (8.17)$$

Since we are concerned only with processes whose termination is remote, we may use the asymptotic expression (Eq. 8.25) for $v_i(t)$

$$v_i(t) = t g_i + v_i \qquad \text{for large } t \qquad (8.25)$$

and transform Eqs. 8.17 into

$$g_i = q_i + \sum_{j=1}^{N} a_{ij}(t g_j + v_j)$$

or

$$g_i = q_i + t \sum_{j=1}^{N} a_{ij} g_j + \sum_{j=1}^{N} a_{ij} v_j \qquad i = 1, 2, \cdots, N \qquad (8.26)$$

If Eqs. 8.26 are to hold for all large t, then we obtain the two sets of linear algebraic equations

$$\sum_{j=1}^{N} a_{ij} g_j = 0 \qquad i = 1, 2, \cdots, N \qquad (8.27)$$

$$g_i = q_i + \sum_{j=1}^{N} a_{ij} v_j \qquad i = 1, 2, \cdots, N \qquad (8.28)$$

Equations 8.27 and 8.28 are analogous to Eqs. 6.3 and 6.4 for the discrete-time process. Solution of Eqs. 8.27 expresses the gain of each state in terms of the gains of the recurrent chains in the process.

The relative value of one state in each chain is set equal to zero, and Eqs. 8.28 are used to solve for the remaining relative values and the gains of the recurrent chains.

The Policy-Improvement Routine

Suppose that we have a policy that is optimal when t units of time remain, and that this policy has expected total rewards $v_i(t)$. If we are considering what policy to follow if more time than t is available, we see from Eqs. 8.17 that we may maximize our rate of increase of $v_i(t)$ by maximizing

$$q_i^k + \sum_{j=1}^{N} a_{ij}^k v_j(t) \tag{8.29}$$

with respect to the alternatives k in state i. If t is large, we may use $v_j(t) = t g_j + v_j$ to obtain

$$q_i^k + \sum_{j=1}^{N} a_{ij}^k (t g_j + v_j)$$

or

$$q_i^k + \sum_{j=1}^{N} a_{ij}^k v_j + t \sum_{j=1}^{N} a_{ij}^k g_j \tag{8.30}$$

as the quantity to be maximized in the ith state. For large t, Expression 8.30 is maximized by the alternative that maximizes

$$\sum_{j=1}^{N} a_{ij}^k g_j \tag{8.31}$$

the gain test quantity, using the gains of the old policy. However, when all alternatives produce the same value of Expression 8.31 or when a group of alternatives produces the same maximum value, then the tie is broken by the alternative that maximizes

$$q_i^k + \sum_{j=1}^{N} a_{ij}^k v_j \tag{8.32}$$

the value test quantity, using the relative values of the old policy. The relative values may be used for the value test because a constant difference will not affect decisions within a chain.

The general iteration cycle is shown in Fig. 8.1. It corresponds completely with Fig. 6.1 for the discrete-time case and has a completely analogous proof. The rules for starting and stopping the process are unchanged.

Policy Evaluation

Use a_{ij} and q_i for a given policy to solve the double set of equations

$$\sum_{j=1}^{N} a_{ij} g_j = 0 \qquad i = 1, 2, \cdots, N$$

$$g_i = q_i + \sum_{j=1}^{N} a_{ij} v_j \qquad i = 1, 2, \cdots, N$$

for all v_i and g_i, by setting the value of one v_i in each recurrent chain to zero.

Policy Improvement

For each state i, determine the alternative k that maximizes

$$\sum_{j=1}^{N} a_{ij}{}^k g_j$$

using the gains g_j of the previous policy, and make it the new decision in the ith state.
If

$$\sum_{j=1}^{N} a_{ij}{}^k g_j$$

is the same for all alternatives, or if several alternatives are equally good according to this test, the decision must be made on the basis of relative values rather than gains. Therefore, if the gain test fails, break the tie by determining the alternative k that maximizes

$$q_i{}^k + \sum_{j=1}^{N} a_{ij}{}^k v_j$$

using the relative values of the previous policy, and by making it the new decision in the ith state.

Regardless of whether the policy-improvement test is based on gains or values, if the old decision in the ith state yields as high a value of the test quantity as any other alternative, leave the old decision unchanged. This rule assures convergence in the case of equivalent policies.

When this procedure has been repeated for all states, a new policy has been determined, and new $[a_{ij}]$ and $[q_i]$ matrices have been obtained. If the new policy is the same as the previous one, the iteration process has converged, and the best policy has been found; otherwise, enter the upper box.

Fig. 8.1. General iteration cycle for continuous-time decision processes.

Completely Ergodic Processes

If, as is usually the case, all possible policies of the problem are completely ergodic, the computational process may be considerably simplified. Since all states of each Markov process have the same gain g, the value-determination operation involves only the solution of the equations

$$g = q_i + \sum_{j=1}^{N} a_{ij} v_j \qquad i = 1, 2, \cdots, N \tag{8.33}$$

with v_N set equal to zero. The solution for g and the remaining v_i is then used to find an improved policy. Multiplication of Eqs. 8.33 by the limiting state probability π_i and summation over i show that

$$g = \sum_{i=1}^{N} \pi_i q_i$$

a result previously obtained.

The policy-improvement routine becomes simply: For each state i, find the alternative k that maximizes

$$q_i^k + \sum_{j=1}^{N} a_{ij}^k v_j$$

using the relative values of the previous policy. This alternative becomes the new decision in the ith state. A new policy has been found when this procedure has been performed for every state.

The iteration cycle for completely ergodic continuous-time systems is shown in Fig. 8.2. It is completely analogous to that shown in Fig. 4.2 for discrete-time processes. Note that, if the iteration is started in the policy-improvement routine with all $v_i = 0$, the initial policy selected is the one that maximizes the earning rate of each state. This policy is analogous to the policy of maximizing expected immediate reward for discrete-time processes.

The proof of the properties of the iteration cycle for the continuous-time case is very close to the proof for discrete time. We shall illustrate this remark by the proof of policy improvement for the iteration cycle of Fig. 8.2.

Consider two policies, A and B. The policy-improvement routine has produced policy B as a successor to policy A. Therefore we know

$$q_i^B + \sum_{j=1}^{N} a_{ij}^B v_j^A \geq q_i^A + \sum_{j=1}^{N} a_{ij}^A v_j^A$$

or

$$\gamma_i = q_i^B + \sum_{j=1}^{N} a_{ij}^B v_j^A - q_i^A \sum_{j=1}^{N} a_{ij}^A v_j^A \tag{8.34}$$

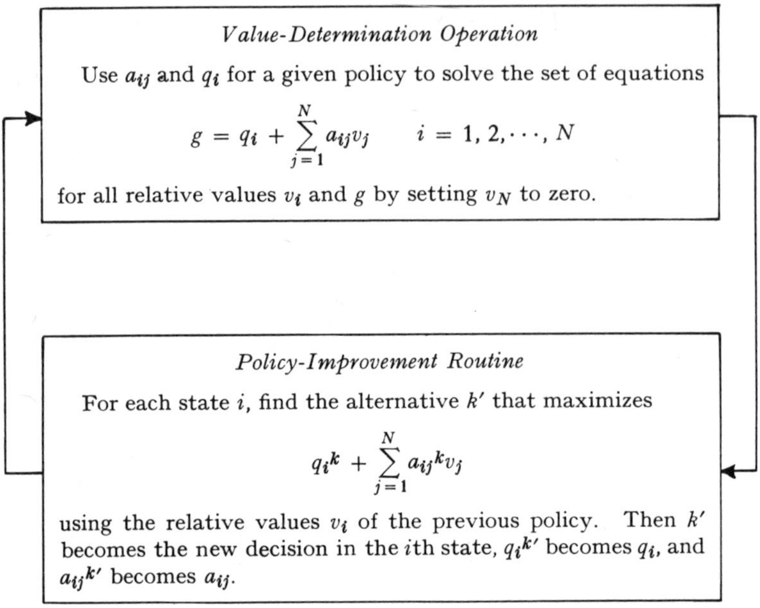

Value-Determination Operation

Use a_{ij} and q_i for a given policy to solve the set of equations

$$g = q_i + \sum_{j=1}^{N} a_{ij} v_j \qquad i = 1, 2, \cdots, N$$

for all relative values v_i and g by setting v_N to zero.

Policy-Improvement Routine

For each state i, find the alternative k' that maximizes

$$q_i{}^k + \sum_{j=1}^{N} a_{ij}{}^k v_j$$

using the relative values v_i of the previous policy. Then k' becomes the new decision in the ith state, $q_i{}^{k'}$ becomes q_i, and $a_{ij}{}^{k'}$ becomes a_{ij}.

Fig. 8.2. Iteration cycle for completely ergodic continuous-time decision processes.

and $\gamma_i \geq 0$. From the equations of the value-determination operation we know

$$g^B = q_i{}^B + \sum_{j=1}^{N} a_{ij}{}^B v_j{}^B \tag{8.35}$$

$$g^A = q_i{}^A + \sum_{j=1}^{N} a_{ij}{}^A v_j{}^A \tag{8.36}$$

If Eq. 8.36 is subtracted from Eq. 8.35 and if Eq. 8.34 is used to eliminate $q_i{}^B - q_i{}^A$, we obtain

$$g^B - g^A = \gamma_i + \sum_{j=1}^{N} a_{ij}{}^B (v_j{}^B - v_j{}^A) \tag{8.37}$$

Let $g^\Delta = g^B - g^A$ and $v_i{}^\Delta = v_i{}^B - v_i{}^A$. Then Eq. 8.37 becomes

$$g^\Delta = \gamma_i + \sum_{j=1}^{N} a_{ij}{}^B v_j{}^\Delta \qquad i = 1, 2, \cdots, N \tag{8.38}$$

Equations 8.38 are the equations of the value-determination operation written in terms of differences rather than absolute values. We know

THE FOREMAN'S DILEMMA

the solution is

$$g^\Delta = \sum_{j=1}^{N} \pi_i^B \gamma_i \qquad (8.39)$$

where π_i^B is the limiting state probability of state i under policy B.

Since all $\pi_i^B \geqslant 0$, and all $\gamma_i \geqslant 0$, therefore $g^\Delta \geqslant 0$. In particular, g^B will be greater than g^A if an improvement in the test quantity

$$q_i^k + \sum_{j=1}^{N} a_{ij}^k v_j$$

can be made in any state i that is recurrent under policy B.

The proof that the iteration cycle must converge on the optimal policy is the same as that given in Chapter 4 for the discrete case.

The Foreman's Dilemma

Let us solve the foreman's problem shown in Table 8.2. Which maintenance service and which repair service will provide greatest earnings per unit time? Since all policies in the system are completely ergodic, the simplified procedure of Fig. 8.2 can be used. Let us choose as our initial policy the one that maximizes the earning rate for each state. This is the policy consisting of normal maintenance and inside repair. For this policy

$$\mathbf{d} = \begin{bmatrix} 1 \\ 1 \end{bmatrix} \qquad \mathbf{A} = \begin{bmatrix} -5 & 5 \\ 4 & -4 \end{bmatrix} \qquad \mathbf{q} = \begin{bmatrix} 6 \\ -3 \end{bmatrix}$$

The value-determination equations (Eqs. 8.33) are

$$g = 6 - 5v_1 + 5v_2 \qquad g = -3 + 4v_1 - 4v_2$$

The solution of these equations with $v_2 = 0$ is

$$g = 1 \qquad v_1 = 1 \qquad v_2 = 0$$

To find a policy with higher gain, we perform the policy-improvement routine as shown in Table 8.3.

Table 8.3. POLICY IMPROVEMENT FOR FOREMAN'S DILEMMA

State i	Alternative k	Test Quantity $q_i^k + \sum_{j=1}^{N} a_{ij}^k v_j$
1	1	$6 - 5(1) = 1$
	2	$4 - 2(1) = 2 \leftarrow$
2	1	$-3 + 4(1) = 1$
	2	$-5 + 7(1) = 2 \leftarrow$

The second alternative in each state is selected as a better policy. It has been found that the policy of using expensive maintenance and outside repair is more profitable than that of using normal services. We evaluate this policy

$$\mathbf{d} = \begin{bmatrix} 2 \\ 2 \end{bmatrix} \qquad \mathbf{A} = \begin{bmatrix} -2 & 2 \\ 7 & -7 \end{bmatrix} \qquad \mathbf{q} = \begin{bmatrix} 4 \\ -5 \end{bmatrix}$$

using Eqs. 8.33. We have

$$g = 4 - 2v_1 + 2v_2 \qquad g = -5 + 7v_1 - 7v_2$$

The solution of these equations with $v_2 = 0$ is

$$g = 2 \qquad v_1 = 1 \qquad v_2 = 0$$

Note that the gain is larger than it was before.

We must now enter the policy-improvement routine to see if we can find a still better policy. However, since the values have coincidentally not been changed, the policy-improvement routine would yield once more the policy $\mathbf{d} = \begin{bmatrix} 2 \\ 2 \end{bmatrix}$. Because this policy has been achieved twice in succession, it must be the optimal policy. Hence, the foreman should use more expensive maintenance and outside repair; in this way he will increase his profits from \$1 to \$2 per hour, on the average. Note that, since $v_1 - v_2 = 1$, the foreman should be willing to pay as much as \$1 for an instantaneous repair. The reader may investigate policies $\mathbf{d} = \begin{bmatrix} 1 \\ 2 \end{bmatrix}$ and $\mathbf{d} = \begin{bmatrix} 2 \\ 1 \end{bmatrix}$ to assure himself that they do have lower earnings per hour than the optimal policy.

Computational Considerations

We have seen that the solution of the continuous-time decision process involves about the same amount of computation as the solution of the corresponding discrete process. As a matter of fact, the two types of processes are computationally equivalent, so that the same computer program may be used for the solution of both. To see this, let us write the value-determination equations (Eqs. 6.3 and 6.4) for the discrete process

$$g_i = \sum_{j=1}^{N} p_{ij} g_j \qquad i = 1, 2, \cdots, N \qquad (6.3)$$

$$g_i + v_i = q_i + \sum_{j=1}^{N} p_{ij} v_j \qquad i = 1, 2, \cdots, N \qquad (6.4)$$

These equations may be written as

$$\sum_{j=1}^{N}(p_{ij}-\delta_{ij})g_j = 0$$

$$g_i = q_i + \sum_{j=1}^{N}(p_{ij}-\delta_{ij})v_j$$

where δ_{ij} is the Kronecker delta; $\delta_{ij} = 1$ if $i = j$ and 0 if $i \neq j$. If we now let $a_{ij} = p_{ij} - \delta_{ij}$, we have

$$\sum_{j=1}^{N} a_{ij}g_j = 0$$

$$g_i = q_i + \sum_{j=1}^{N} a_{ij}v_j$$

These are the value-determination equations (Eqs. 8.27 and 8.28) for the continuous-time decision process. Thus if we have a program for the solution of Eqs. 6.3 and 6.4 for the discrete process, we may use it for the solution of the continuous process described by the matrix **A** by transforming the transition rates to "pseudo" transition probabilities according to the relation $p_{ij} = a_{ij} + \delta_{ij}$.*

As far as the policy-improvement routine is concerned, in the discrete case we maximize either

$$\sum_{j=1}^{N} p_{ij}{}^k g_j \quad \text{or} \quad q_i{}^k + \sum_{j=1}^{N} p_{ij}{}^k v_j$$

with respect to all alternatives k in state i.

Our decisions would be unchanged if we instead maximized

$$\sum_{j=1}^{N}(p_{ij}{}^k - \delta_{ij})g_j \quad \text{or} \quad q_i{}^k + \sum_{j=1}^{N}(p_{ij}{}^k - \delta_{ij})v_j$$

in state i, since only terms dependent upon k affect decisions. In terms of $a_{ij}{}^k = p_{ij}{}^k - \delta_{ij}$, the quantities to be maximized are

$$\sum_{j=1}^{N} a_{ij}{}^k g_j \quad \text{and} \quad q_i{}^k + \sum_{j=1}^{N} a_{ij}{}^k v_j$$

However, these are the test quantities for the policy-improvement routine of the continuous process. As a result, a policy-improvement routine programmed for the discrete process may be used for the continuous process if the transformation $p_{ij}{}^k = a_{ij}{}^k + \delta_{ij}$ is performed.

* If the computer program assumes that $0 \leq p_{ij} \leq 1$, it will be necessary to scale the a_{ij} so that $-1 \leq a_{ii} \leq 0$.

The Continuous-Time Decision Process with Discounting

In Chapter 7 we studied the discrete sequential process with discounting or with an indefinite duration. We may analyze continuous-time decision processes with similar elements by use of an analogous approach. Let us define a discount rate $0 < \alpha < \infty$ in such a way that a unit quantity of money received after a very short time interval dt is now worth $1 - \alpha\, dt$. This definition corresponds to continuous compounding at the rate α. An alternate interpretation of α that allows the process an indefinite duration is that there is a probability $\alpha\, dt$ that the process will terminate in the interval dt.

If $v_i(t)$ is the total expected earnings of the system in time t, then by analogy with Eq. 8.15 we have

$$v_i(t + dt) = (1 - \alpha\, dt)\left\{\left(1 - \sum_{j \neq i} a_{ij}\, dt\right)[r_{ii}\, dt + v_i(t)] + \sum_{j \neq i} a_{ij}\, dt[r_{ij} + v_j(t)]\right\} \quad (8.40)$$

In this equation we assume that rewards are paid at the end of the interval dt and that the process receives no reward from termination. Using the definition given by Eq. 8.2, we may rewrite Eq. 8.40 as

$$v_i(t + dt) = (1 - \alpha\, dt)\left\{(1 + a_{ii}\, dt)[r_{ii}\, dt + v_i(t)] + \sum_{j \neq i} a_{ij}\, dt[r_{ij} + v_j(t)]\right\}$$

or

$$v_i(t + dt) = (1 - \alpha\, dt)\left[\left(r_{ii} + \sum_{j \neq i} a_{ij} r_{ij}\right) dt + v_i(t) + \sum_{j=1}^{N} a_{ij}\, dt\, v_j(t)\right]$$

and

$$v_i(t + dt) = \left(r_{ii} + \sum_{j \neq i} a_{ij} r_{ij}\right) dt + v_i(t) + \sum_{j=1}^{N} a_{ij}\, dt\, v_j(t) - \alpha\, dt\, v_i(t)$$

where terms of higher order than dt have been neglected.

Introduction of the earning rate from Eq. 8.16 and rearrangement yield

$$v_i(t + dt) - v_i(t) + \alpha\, dt\, v_i(t) = q_i\, dt + \sum_{j=1}^{N} a_{ij}\, dt\, v_j(t)$$

CONTINUOUS-TIME DECISION PROCESS WITH DISCOUNTING

If this equation is divided by dt and the limit taken as dt approaches zero, we have

$$\frac{dv_i(t)}{dt} + \alpha v_i(t) = q_i + \sum_{j=1}^{N} a_{ij} v_j(t) \qquad i = 1, 2, \cdots, N \qquad (8.41)$$

Equations 8.41 are analogous to Eqs. 8.17 and reduce to them if $\alpha = 0$. In vector form, Eqs. 8.41 become

$$\frac{d\mathbf{v}(t)}{dt} + \alpha \mathbf{v}(t) = \mathbf{q} + \mathbf{A}\mathbf{v}(t) \qquad (8.42)$$

Since Eq. 8.42 is a linear constant-coefficient differential equation, we should expect a Laplace transformation to be useful. If the transform of Eq. 8.42 is taken, we obtain

$$\mathbf{v}s(s) - \mathbf{v}(0) + \alpha \mathbf{v}(s) = \frac{1}{s}\mathbf{q} + \mathbf{A}\mathbf{v}(s)$$

or

$$[(s + \alpha)\mathbf{I} - \mathbf{A}]\mathbf{v}(s) = \frac{1}{s}\mathbf{q} + \mathbf{v}(0)$$

and finally

$$\mathbf{v}(s) = \frac{1}{s}[(s + \alpha)\mathbf{I} - \mathbf{A}]^{-1}\mathbf{q} + [(s + \alpha)\mathbf{I} - \mathbf{A}]^{-1}\mathbf{v}(0) \qquad (8.43)$$

We might use Eq. 8.43 and inverse transformation to find $\mathbf{v}(t)$ for a given process. As usual, however, we are interested in processes of long duration, so that only the asymptotic form of $\mathbf{v}(t)$ for large t interests us. Let us recall from Eq. 8.11 that

$$(s\mathbf{I} - \mathbf{A})^{-1} = \frac{1}{s}\mathbf{S} + \mathcal{T}(s) \qquad (8.11)$$

where $\mathbf{S}$ is the matrix of limiting state probabilities and $\mathcal{T}(s)$ is a matrix consisting of only transient components. It follows that

$$[(s + \alpha)\mathbf{I} - \mathbf{A}]^{-1} = \frac{1}{s + \alpha}\mathbf{S} + \mathcal{T}(s + \alpha) \qquad (8.44)$$

so that $[(s + \alpha)\mathbf{I} - \mathbf{A}]^{-1}$ has *all* transient components. If Eq. 8.44 is used in Eq. 8.43, we have

$$\mathbf{v}(s) = \frac{1}{s}\left[\frac{1}{s + \alpha}\mathbf{S} + \mathcal{T}(s + \alpha)\right]\mathbf{q} + \left[\frac{1}{s + \alpha}\mathbf{S} + \mathcal{T}(s + \alpha)\right]\mathbf{v}(0) \qquad (8.45)$$

We now wish to know which components of $\mathbf{v}(t)$ will be nonzero for large t. The matrix multiplying $\mathbf{q}$ contains a step component of magnitude $[(1/\alpha)\mathbf{S} + \mathcal{T}(\alpha)]$; all other terms of Eq. 8.45 represent transient components of $\mathbf{v}(t)$. Therefore, if we define a vector $\mathbf{v}$ of present values v_i so that

$$\mathbf{v} = \lim_{t \to \infty} \mathbf{v}(t)$$

we have

$$\mathbf{v} = \left[\frac{1}{\alpha}\mathbf{S} + \mathscr{T}(\alpha)\right]\mathbf{q}$$

or

$$\mathbf{v} = (\alpha\mathbf{I} - \mathbf{A})^{-1}\mathbf{q} \tag{8.46}$$

using Eq. 8.11.

The vector $\mathbf{v}$ represents the discounted future earnings in a very long time if the system is started in each state. Equation 8.46 shows how these present values are related to the discount rate α, the transition-rate matrix $\mathbf{A}$, and the earning-rate vector $\mathbf{q}$. Equation 8.46 may also be written in the form

$$\alpha v_i = q_i + \sum_{j=1}^{N} a_{ij}v_j \qquad i = 1, 2, \cdots, N \tag{8.47}$$

We may solve Eqs. 8.47 to find the present values of any continuous-time decision process with discounting.

Policy Improvement

We are interested not only in evaluating a given policy but also in finding the policy that has highest present values in all states. We should like to be able to solve a problem such as that posed by Table 8.2 when discounting is an important element. Equations 8.47 constitute a value-determination operation; we still require a policy-improvement routine.

If we desired to maximize the rate of growth of $v_i(t)$ at time t in Eq. 8.41, we should maximize

$$q_i^k + \sum_{j=1}^{N} a_{ij}^k v_j(t) - \alpha v_i(t)$$

with respect to all the alternatives k in the ith state. If we are interested only in large t, we may use the asymptotic present value v_i rather than $v_i(t)$ to obtain the test quantity

$$q_i^k + \sum_{j=1}^{N} a_{ij}^k v_j - \alpha v_i$$

POLICY IMPROVEMENT

However, since v_i does not depend upon k, the expression

$$q_i^k + \sum_{j=1}^{N} a_{ij}^k v_j$$

is a sufficient test quantity to be maximized with respect to all alternatives k in state i.

The policy-improvement routine is thus: For each state i, find the alternative k that maximizes

$$q_i^k + \sum_{j=1}^{N} a_{ij}^k v_j$$

using the present values of the previous policy. This alternative becomes the new decision in the ith state. When the procedure has been repeated for all states, a new policy has been determined. This new policy must have present values that are greater than those of the previous policy unless the two policies are identical. In the latter case the optimal policy has been found.

The value-determination operation and the policy-improvement routine are shown in the iteration cycle of Fig. 8.3. The rules for entering and leaving the cycle are the same as those given for earlier cases. We shall now prove the properties of the cycle, following the lines of the proof for the discrete case given in Chapter 7.

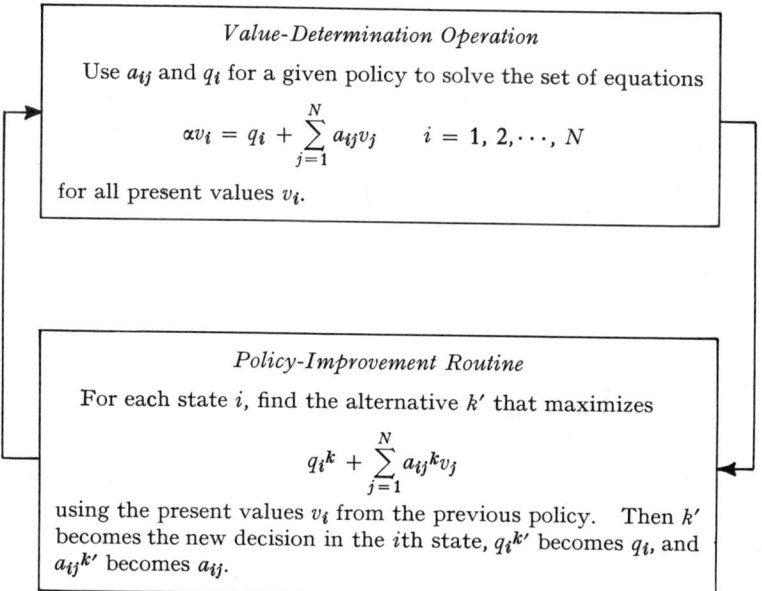

Fig. 8.3. Iteration cycle for continuous-time decision processes with discounting.

Suppose that the iteration cycle produces a policy B as a successor to policy A. Since B followed A, we know that

$$q_i^B + \sum_{j=1}^{N} a_{ij}^B v_j^A \geq q_i^A + \sum_{j=1}^{N} a_{ij}^A v_j^A \quad \text{in every state } i.$$

Equivalently,

$$\gamma_i = q_i^B + \sum_{j=1}^{N} a_{ij}^B v_j^A - q_i^A - \sum_{j=1}^{N} a_{ij}^A v_j^A \geq 0 \quad \text{for all } i$$

where γ_i is the improvement in the test quantity that the policy-improvement routine was able to achieve in the ith state. For the individual policies the value-determination operation yields

$$\alpha v_i^A = q_i^A + \sum_{j=1}^{N} a_{ij}^A v_j^A$$

$$\alpha v_i^B = q_i^B + \sum_{j=1}^{N} a_{ij}^B v_j^B$$

If the first equation is subtracted from the second and the relation for γ_i is used to eliminate $q_i^B - q_i^A$, we obtain

$$\alpha(v_i^B - v_i^A) = \gamma_i + \sum_{j=1}^{N} a_{ij}^B (v_j^B - v_j^A)$$

or

$$\alpha v_i^\Delta = \gamma_i + \sum_{j=1}^{N} a_{ij}^B v_j^\Delta$$

where $v_i^\Delta = v_i^B - v_i^A$. These equations are the same as our value-determination equations except that they are written in terms of differences in present values. In vector form their solution is

$$\mathbf{v}^\Delta = (\alpha \mathbf{I} - \mathbf{A})^{-1} \boldsymbol{\gamma}$$

where $\boldsymbol{\gamma}$ is the vector with components γ_i. All elements of $(\alpha \mathbf{I} - \mathbf{A})^{-1}$ are nonnegative, as were those of $(\mathbf{I} - \beta \mathbf{P})^{-1}$ in the discrete case, again on either physical or mathematical grounds. If any $\gamma_i > 0$, at least one v_i^Δ must be greater than zero and no v_i^Δ can be less than zero. The policy-improvement routine must increase the present values of at least one state and can decrease the present value of no state.

Similarly, no policy B that has some higher present values than policy A can remain undiscovered because of convergence on A. This is true because in such a case all γ_i would be ≤ 0, while at least one v_i^Δ would be > 0; this situation would contradict the relation derived above. When the iteration cycle has converged on a policy, that policy has higher present values than any other nonequivalent policy.

An Example

Let us use our results to solve the sequential decision problem presented in Table 8.2 with $\alpha = \frac{1}{9}$. We may interpret this to mean that the duration of the foreman's operation is exponentially distributed with mean 9 hours, or we may think of some investment situation in which the interest rate is important. As is the custom, we shall choose as our initial policy the one that maximizes earning rate; that is,

$$\mathbf{d} = \begin{bmatrix} 1 \\ 1 \end{bmatrix} \qquad \mathbf{A} = \begin{bmatrix} -5 & 5 \\ 4 & -4 \end{bmatrix} \qquad \mathbf{q} = \begin{bmatrix} 6 \\ -3 \end{bmatrix}$$

The value-determination equations (Eqs. 8.47) are

$$\tfrac{1}{9}v_1 = 6 - 5v_1 + 5v_2 \qquad \tfrac{1}{9}v_2 = -3 + 4v_1 - 4v_2$$

Their solution is

$$v_1 = \tfrac{783}{82} \qquad v_2 = \tfrac{702}{82}$$

Proceeding to find a better policy, we employ the policy-improvement routine as shown in Table 8.4.

Table 8.4. First Policy Improvement for Foreman's Dilemma with Discounting

State i	Alternative k	Test Quantity $q_i^k + \sum_{j=1}^{N} a_{ij}^k v_j$
1	1	$6 - 5(\tfrac{783}{82}) + 5(\tfrac{702}{82}) = \tfrac{87}{82}$
	2	$4 - 2(\tfrac{783}{82}) + 2(\tfrac{702}{82}) = \tfrac{166}{82}$ ←
2	1	$-3 + 4(\tfrac{783}{82}) - 4(\tfrac{702}{82}) = \tfrac{78}{82}$
	2	$-5 + 7(\tfrac{783}{82}) - 7(\tfrac{702}{82}) = \tfrac{157}{82}$ ←

The second alternative in each state constitutes a better policy, so that now

$$\mathbf{d} = \begin{bmatrix} 2 \\ 2 \end{bmatrix} \qquad \mathbf{A} = \begin{bmatrix} -2 & 2 \\ 7 & -7 \end{bmatrix} \qquad \mathbf{q} = \begin{bmatrix} 4 \\ -5 \end{bmatrix}$$

The value-determination equations (Eqs. 8.47) are

$$\tfrac{1}{9}v_1 = 4 - 2v_1 + 2v_2 \qquad \tfrac{1}{9}v_2 = -5 + 7v_1 - 7v_2$$

Their solution is

$$v_1 = \tfrac{1494}{82} \qquad v_2 = \tfrac{1413}{82}$$

120   THE CONTINUOUS-TIME DECISION PROCESS

Note that the present values have once more increased. The policy-improvement routine is entered again, with results shown in Table 8.5.

Table 8.5.   Second Policy Improvement for Foreman's Dilemma with Discounting

State i	Alternative k	Test Quantity $q_i{}^k + \sum a_{ij}{}^k v_j$
1	1	$\frac{87}{82}$
	2	$\frac{166}{82}$ ←
2	1	$\frac{78}{82}$
	2	$\frac{157}{82}$ ←

Since $v_1 - v_2$ has remained unchanged, the values for the test quantities are the same as those in Table 8.4. The policy $\mathbf{d} = \begin{bmatrix} 2 \\ 2 \end{bmatrix}$ has been found twice in succession. Therefore, it is the optimal policy; it has higher present values in all states than any other policy. Even when the expected duration of the process is only 9 hours, the foreman should use expensive maintenance and outside repair.

Comparison with Discrete-Time Case

In the discrete sequential decision process with discounting the value-determination equations are

$$v_i = q_i + \beta \sum_{j=1}^{N} p_{ij} v_j \qquad i = 1, 2, \cdots, N \qquad (7.9)$$

If we have developed a computer program for this operation, we might be interested in knowing whether such a program would be useful in the continuous case. For the continuous case the analogous equations are

$$\alpha v_i = q_i' + \sum_{j=1}^{N} a_{ij} v_j \qquad i = 1, 2, \cdots, N \qquad (8.48)$$

where q_i' has been used to distinguish the continuous from the discrete case. We may define $a_{ij} = p_{ij} - \delta_{ij}$ and write Eq. 8.48 as

$$\alpha v_i = q_i' + \sum_{j=1}^{N} (p_{ij} - \delta_{ij}) v_j$$

or

$$(1 + \alpha) v_i = q_i' + \sum_{j=1}^{N} p_{ij} v_j$$

COMPARISON WITH DISCRETE-TIME CASE

and

$$v_i = \frac{1}{1+\alpha} q_i' + \frac{1}{1+\alpha} \sum_{j=1}^{N} p_{ij} v_j$$

If we define $\beta = 1/(1+\alpha)$ and $q_i = 1/(1+\alpha)q_i'$, then we have

$$v_i = q_i + \beta \sum_{j=1}^{N} p_{ij} v_j$$

a set of equations of the same form as those for the discrete case. Thus if we have a continuous problem described by α, $\mathbf{q'}$, and $\mathbf{A}$, we may use the program for the discrete problem described by β, $\mathbf{q}$, and $\mathbf{P}$ by making the transformations

$$\beta = \frac{1}{1+\alpha} \qquad \mathbf{q} = \beta \mathbf{q'} \qquad \mathbf{P} = \mathbf{A} + \mathbf{I}$$

In the policy-improvement routine for the discrete case, the test quantity is

$$q_i^k + \beta \sum_{j=1}^{N} p_{ij}^k v_j$$

For the continuous case it is

$$q_i'^k + \sum_{j=1}^{N} a_{ij}^k v_j$$

This quantity may be rewritten as

$$q_i'^k + \sum_{j=1}^{N} (p_{ij}^k - \delta_{ij}) v_j$$

where $a_{ij}^k = p_{ij}^k - \delta_{ij}$. We now have an expression equivalent to

$$q_i'^k + \sum_{j=1}^{N} p_{ij}^k v_j$$

since v_j does not depend on k. If $q_i'^k = (1/\beta) q_i^k$, where $\beta = 1/(1+\alpha)$, then we have

$$\frac{1}{\beta} q_i^k + \sum_{j=1}^{N} p_{ij}^k v_j$$

and this of course, is proportional to

$$q_i^k + \beta \sum_{j=1}^{N} p_{ij}^k v_j$$

which is the test quantity for the discrete case. Thus the same transformation that allowed us to use a program for the discrete case in the solution of the value-determination operation allows us to use a program for the policy-improvement routine that is based upon the discrete process.

We see that by suitable transformations a single program suffices for both the discrete and continuous cases with discounting. Since we showed the same relation earlier for cases without discounting, it is clear that the continuous-time decision process, with or without discounting, is computationally equivalent to its discrete counterpart.

9

Conclusion

With the discussion of continuous-time processes we have completed our present investigation of dynamic programming and Markov processes. We have seen that the analysis of discrete-time and continuous-time Markov processes is very similar. In the discrete case the z-transform is a powerful analytic technique, whereas for the continuous case the Laplace transform assumes this role. In either situation the pertinent transformation has allowed us to analyze the special cases of periodicity and multiple chains that so often complicate other analytic approaches.

Even when a structure of rewards is added to the process, the transformational methods are useful for calculating total expected rewards as a function of time and for determining the asymptotic forms of the reward expressions. For a system operating under a fixed policy, a knowledge of the total expected rewards of the process constitutes a complete understanding of the system.

The most interesting case arises when there are alternatives available for the operation of the system. In general, we should like to find which set of alternatives or policy will yield the maximum total expected reward. If we are dealing with a discrete system, and if we wish to maximize the total expected reward over only a few stages of the process, then a value-iteration approach is indicated. If, however, we expect the process to have an indefinite duration, the policy-iteration method is preferable. This method will find the policy that has a higher average return per transition than any other policy under consideration. Even in processes with possible multiple-chain behavior, no serious difficulties arise. The computational scheme involved is simple, practical, and easily implemented.

If, however, we are interested in maximizing total expected reward for a continuous-time system, our choice is more limited. The continuous analogue of the value-iteration approach is so laborious that practicality forces us to make simplifications. If we are especially interested in processes of short duration, then the easiest course is to approximate the continuous-time process by a discrete-time process and then use value-iteration. If, on the other hand, we are interested in processes of long duration, the policy-iteration method is just as applicable as it was in the discrete-time case. Furthermore, the computational requirements of the two types of processes are so similar that the same general computer program will suffice for the solution of both classes of problems. We may conclude that the policy-iteration method is especially important in the solution of continuous-time processes because of the lack of practical alternatives.

We have found that the presence of discounting does not change the basic nature of the decision-making problem. The earlier remarks comparing value- and policy-iteration methods for discrete- and continuous-time processes apply with equal weight when discounting is present. The existence of discounting does have some interesting features, however. First, for processes of long duration the concept of gain is replaced by that of present value, and our objective in policy improvement is to maximize the present values of all states. Second, the chain structure of the process can be ignored in our computations. Third, there will exist regions of discount-factor values that have the same optimal policy. These features, however, change our computational procedure very little. A well-designed computer program can solve both discrete- and continuous-time processes, with or without discounting.

Whenever the policy-iteration method is applied, a by-product of the calculation of the optimal policy is a set of state values that permits the evaluation of departures from this policy in special circumstances. In most systems these values are more interesting and useful than their origin might indicate. It is important to remember in using these numbers that their validity rests on the assumption that the optimal policy is being followed almost always.

The examples in baseball strategy, automobile replacement, and so forth, that have been presented are so simplified that they only whet the appetite for further applications. The considerations involved in selecting possible applications are these. First, can the system be adequately described by a number of states small enough to make the solution of the corresponding simultaneous equations computationally feasible? Second, are the data necessary to describe the alternatives of the system available? If the answers to these questions are affirmative, then a possible application has been discovered. There is every reason to believe that a possible application when combined with diligent work will yield a successful application.

Appendix:
The Relationship of Transient to Recurrent Behavior

In the value-determination operation for a completely ergodic process, we must solve the following equation for the v_i and the g:

$$g + v_i = q_i + \sum_{j=1}^{N} p_{ij} v_j \qquad i = 1, 2, \cdots, N \qquad (4.1)$$

Rearranging, we have

$$v_i - \sum_{j=1}^{N} p_{ij} v_j + g = q_i$$

When $v_N = 0$, arbitrarily, then

$$\sum_{j=1}^{N-1} (\delta_{ij} - p_{ij}) v_j + g = q_i \qquad \begin{array}{l} \delta_{ij} = 0 \text{ if } i \neq j \\ \delta_{ij} = 1 \text{ if } i = j \end{array} \qquad (A.1)$$

If we define a matrix

$$\mathbf{M} = [m_{ij}] \qquad \begin{array}{l} m_{ij} = \delta_{ij} - p_{ij} \quad \text{for } j < N \\ m_{iN} = 1 \end{array}$$

then

$$\mathbf{M} = \begin{bmatrix} 1 - p_{11} & -p_{12} & \cdots & -p_{1,N-1} & 1 \\ -p_{21} & 1 - p_{22} & & & 1 \\ \vdots & & & & \vdots \\ -p_{N1} & -p_{N2} & \cdots & -p_{N,N-1} & 1 \end{bmatrix}$$

Note that the matrix **M** is formed by taking the **P** matrix, making all elements negative, adding ones to the main diagonal, and replacing the last column by ones.

If we also define a vector $\tilde{\mathbf{v}}$ where

$$\tilde{v}_i = v_i \qquad i < N$$
$$\tilde{v}_N = g$$

then

$$\tilde{\mathbf{v}} = \begin{bmatrix} v_1 \\ v_2 \\ \vdots \\ v_{N-1} \\ g \end{bmatrix}$$

Equation A.1 in the v_i and the g can then be written in matrix form as

$$\mathbf{M}\tilde{\mathbf{v}} = \mathbf{q}$$

or

$$\tilde{\mathbf{v}} = \mathbf{M}^{-1}\mathbf{q} \tag{A.2}$$

where **q** is the vector of expected immediate rewards. The matrix $\mathbf{M}^{-1}$ will exist if the system is completely ergodic, as we have assumed. Thus, by inverting **M** to obtain $\mathbf{M}^{-1}$ and then postmultiplying $\mathbf{M}^{-1}$ by **q**, v_i for $1 \leq i \leq N - 1$ and g will be determined.

Suppose that state N is a recurrent state and a trapping state, so that $p_{Nj} = 0$ for $j \neq N$, and $p_{NN} = 1$. Furthermore, let there be no recurrent states among the remaining $N - 1$ states of the problem. We know that

$$\tilde{\mathbf{v}} = \mathbf{M}^{-1}\mathbf{q}$$

where **M** assumes the special form

$$\mathbf{M} = \begin{bmatrix} 1 - p_{11} & -p_{12} & \cdots & -p_{1,N-1} & 1 \\ -p_{21} & 1 - p_{22} & & & 1 \\ \vdots & & & & \vdots \\ -p_{N-1,1} & -p_{N-1,2} & \cdots & 1 - p_{N-1,N-1} & 1 \\ \hline 0 & 0 & \cdots & 0 & 1 \end{bmatrix}$$

Let **M** be partitioned as follows:

$$\mathbf{M} = \left[\begin{array}{c|c} \mathbf{W} & \mathbf{f} \\ \hline 0 \ 0 \ \cdots \ 0 & 1 \end{array}\right]$$

RELATIONSHIP OF TRANSIENT TO RECURRENT BEHAVIOR

where the nature of **W** and **f** are evident by comparison with the **M** defined above. From the relations for partitioned matrices we have

$$\mathbf{M}^{-1} = \left[\begin{array}{ccc|c} & \mathbf{W}^{-1} & & -\mathbf{W}^{-1}\mathbf{f} \\ \hline 0 & 0 \cdots & 0 & 1 \end{array} \right]$$

It is clear that $\mathbf{MM}^{-1} = \mathbf{M}^{-1}\mathbf{M} = \mathbf{I}$ as required. The nature of **f** shows us that the elements in the first $N - 1$ rows of the last column of $\mathbf{M}^{-1}$ are each equal to the negative sum of the first $N - 1$ elements in each row. Also, from Eq. A.2, $g = q_N$ as expected.

What is the significance of $\mathbf{W}^{-1}$ and $\mathbf{W}^{-1}\mathbf{f}$? Let us consider the relations for the number of times the system enters each transient state before it is absorbed by the recurrent state. Let u_{ij} equal the expected number of times that a system started in state i will enter state j before it enters state N.

The balancing relations for the u_i are

$$u_{ij} = \sum_{k=1}^{N-1} u_{ik} p_{kj} + \delta_{ij} \qquad i, j \leq N - 1 \qquad (A.3)$$

Equation A.3 may be developed as follows: The number of times a state j will be occupied for a given starting state i depends primarily on its probabilistic relations with other states. For example, if the system spends an average amount of time u_{ik} in some state k and if a fraction p_{kj} of the times state k is occupied a transition is made to state j, then the expected number of transitions into state j from state k is $u_{ik} p_{kj}$. This contribution to u_{ij} must be summed over all of the N states with the exception of the trapping state, and so we have the first term of Eq. A.3. In addition to this mechanism, however, u_{ij} will be increased by 1 if j is the state i in which the system is started; this accounts for the δ_{ij} term of Eq. A.3.

Let us define an $N - 1$ by $N - 1$ square matrix U with components u_{ij}. Then if we write Eq. A.3 in the form

$$\sum_{k=1}^{N-1} u_{ik}(\delta_{kj} - p_{kj}) = \delta_{ij}$$

we see that we have in matrix form

$$\mathbf{UW} = \mathbf{I}$$

or

$$\mathbf{W}^{-1} = \mathbf{U}$$

That is, the matrix $\mathbf{W}^{-1}$ is the matrix $\mathbf{U}$ of average times spent in each state for each starting state. Since these quantities must be nonnegative, the elements of $\mathbf{W}^{-1}$ are nonnegative.

The matrix $\mathbf{W}$ or $\mathbf{U}^{-1}$ has the form of the matrix $[^{L+1}\mathbf{I} - {}^{L+1,\,L+1}\mathbf{P}]$ used in Eq. 6.23 of Chapter 6. Here we would interpret the u_{ij} as the expected number of times the system will enter one of the transient states j in the group $L + 1$ before it enters some recurrent chain if it is started in state i of the group $L + 1$. With this definition, the elements of $[^{L+1}\mathbf{I} - {}^{L+1,\,L+1}\mathbf{P}]^{-1}$ must all be nonnegative by the same argument given here.

Using $\mathbf{W}^{-1} = \mathbf{U}$, Eq. A.2, and the partitioned form of $\mathbf{M}^{-1}$, we may write

$$v_i = \sum_{j=1}^{N-1} u_{ij} q_j - q_N \sum_{j=1}^{N-1} u_{ij} \qquad 1 \leqslant i \leqslant N-1$$

or

$$v_i = \sum_{j=1}^{N-1} u_{ij} q_j - g \sum_{j=1}^{N-1} u_{ij} \qquad 1 \leqslant i \leqslant N-1 \qquad (A.4)$$

The v_i may now be interpreted in the following way. The v_i represent the sum of the expected number of times the system will enter each state j multiplied by the expected immediate reward in that state less the total number of times any state other than N will be entered multiplied by the gain for state N, all given that the system started in state i.

In particular, if the reward q_N in the recurrent state is zero, and if all $q_i \geqslant 0$ for $1 \leqslant i \leqslant N-1$, then

$$v_i = \sum_{j=1}^{N} u_{ij} q_j \geqslant 0 \qquad 1 \leqslant i \leqslant N-1$$

This was exactly the situation encountered in the baseball example of Chapter 5, where we found that no negative values occurred relative to the recurrent state.

Suppose that we are investigating various policies for a system that has only one recurrent state, state N. Suppose further that we have at some stage found a policy B as a successor to policy A. Equation 4.11 must hold for the changes in gain and values

$$g^\Delta + v_i^\Delta = \gamma_i + \sum_{j=1}^{N} p_{ij}{}^B v_j^\Delta \qquad i = 1, 2, \cdots, N \qquad (4.11)$$

Since for this particular system we know that these equations are equivalent to Eq. A.4,

$$v_i^\Delta = \sum_{j=1}^{N} u_{ij}{}^B \gamma_i - g^\Delta \sum_{j=1}^{N} u_{ij}{}^B \qquad i = 1, 2, \cdots, N-1$$

If there has been no change in gain between A and B, then $g^\Delta = 0$, and we have left the sum of nonnegative terms so that v_i^Δ must be nonnegative. We thus see that when increases in gain are not possible the policy-improvement routine will attempt to maximize the values of the transient states. This is the behavior observed in the baseball problem, where at first glance it appeared as if we were violating our ground rules by working with a system in which the gain was zero for all policies.

If the words "recurrent chain with gain g" are substituted for "single recurrent state," the preceding development is virtually unchanged. The policy-improvement routine will not only maximize the gain of a recurrent chain, it will also maximize the values of transient states that run into that chain.

References

1. R. Bellman, *Dynamic Programming*, Princeton University Press, Princeton, N.J., 1957, Chapter XI.
2. M. F. Gardner and J. L. Barnes, *Transients in Linear Systems*, John Wiley & Sons, New York, 1942.
3. R. W. Sittler, "Systems Analysis of Discrete Markov Processes," *IRE Trans. on Circuit Theory*, **CT-3**, No. 1, 257 (1956).
4. Operations Research Center, M.I.T., *Notes on Operations Research 1959*, Technology Press, Cambridge, 1959, Chapters 3, 5, 7.

General References

E. F. Beckenbach, Ed., *Modern Mathematics for the Engineer*, McGraw-Hill Book Company, New York, 1956.

R. Bellman, "A Markovian Decision Process," *J. Math. and Mech.*, **6**, 679 (1957).

J. L. Doob, *Stochastic Processes*, John Wiley & Sons, New York, 1953.

G. Elving, "Zur Theorie der Markoffschen Ketten," *Acta Soc. Sci. Fennicae*, **2**, No. 8, 1937.

W. Feller, *An Introduction to Probability Theory and Its Applications*, Vol. I, 2nd Ed., John Wiley & Sons, New York, 1957.

B. Friedman, *Principles and Techniques of Applied Mathematics*, John Wiley & Sons, New York, 1956.

W. H. Huggins, "Signal-Flow Graphs and Random Signals," *Proc. I.R.E.*, **45**, 74 (1957).

J. G. Kemeny and J. L. Snell, *Finite Markov Chains*, D. Van Nostrand Company, Princeton, 1960.

V. I. Romanovskii, *Diskretnye Tsepi Markova*, State Publishers, Moscow, 1949.

T. A. Sarymsakov, *Osnovy Teorii Protsessov Markova*, State Publishers, Moscow, 1954.

Index

Alternatives, 26–28, 33, 104, 105

Barnes, J. L., 94
Baseball problem, best long-run policy, 52
 computational requirements, 52
 evaluation of base situations, 53
Bellman, R., 1, 29

Car problem, best long-run policy, 57, 58, 89, 90
 computational requirements, 58, 89
 solution in special situations, 58, 89
Chain, periodic, 15
 recurrent, 13
Computational considerations, 36, 37, 49–52, 112–114, 120–123

Decision, 28, 33, 105
Decision vector, 33
Discount factor, 76
Discount rate, 114

Earning rate, 100
Equivalence of discrete- and continuous-time processes, 96, 112–114, 120–122

Foreman's dilemma, 96–105, 111, 112, 119, 120
Frog example, 3, 17, 18

Gain, changes related to policy changes, 43, 49, 72–75, 111
 of a process, 22, 24, 32, 36, 102
 of a state, 23, 24, 61–63, 103
 in multiple-chain processes, 60–63
Gardner, M. F., 94

Iteration cycle, for continuous-time processes, 108, 110
 for continuous-time processes with discounting, 117
 for discrete-time processes, 38, 64
 for discrete-time processes with discounting, 84
 for multiple-chain processes, 64

Laplace transforms, definition, 94
 of vectors and matrices, 95
 table of, 95

Markov processes, definition, 3, 92
Matrices, differential, 12, 23, 94, 98
 stochastic, 11, 23, 94, 98

Partial-fraction expansion, 10
Policy, 28, 33, 105
 optimal, 28, 33, 61, 81, 105, 116
Policy improvement by a change in chain structure, 68

Present values, 81, 116
   changes related to policy changes, 87, 118
Principle of Optimality, 29
Process, completely ergodic, 6, 13, 24, 32, 60, 98, 109–111
   continuous-time, 3, 92
   discrete-time, 3
   discrete-time related to continuous-time, 96, 98
   finite-state, 3

Relative values, 35, 62, 107
   interpretation of, 35, 41, 112
   sufficiency of, 35, 65
Reward, 17, 76
   expected immediate, 18
   scaling, 36, 37
Reward rate, 99

Stage of a process, 28
State, definition, 3
State probability, 5, 92
   in periodic chains, 16
   limiting, 7, 98, 99
State-probability vector, 5

Taxicab problem, best long-run policy, 48, 87, 88

Total expected reward, for continuous-time processes, 99–104
   for continuous-time processes with discounting, 114–116
   for discrete-time processes, 18
   for discrete-time processes with discounting, 76–79
Total-value vector, 18, 21
Toymaker example, 4–7, 10, 11, 18–21, 39–42, 80, 84–86
Transient state, 12
Transition, 3
Transition probability, 4
Transition-probability matrix, 4
Transition rate, 92
Transition-rate matrix, 93
Transition reward, 99
Trapping state, 12

Value iteration, for discrete-time processes, 28–31
   for discrete-time processes with discounting, 80, 81
   limitations, 30, 31

z-transforms, definition, 7
   examples of, 8
   of vectors and matrices, 9
   table of, 9